Micropolis
BBS Primer

Micropolis
BBS Primer

Micropolis Handbooks

Micropolis Press

Micropolis BBS Primer

from the Micropolis Handbooks series

Second, extensively updated edition. Copyright © 2024 Micropolis

Micropolis
www.micropolis.com
webmaster@micropolis.com

Printed in the United States of America
and distributed globally by Ingram Content Group, Tennessee, USA
through Lightning Source LLC and Ingram affiliates and subsidiaries.

Cover art, text and book illustrations copyright © 2024 Micropolis Press
an imprint of publisher Clipland GmbH, Westfaelische Str. 64, 47169 Duisburg, Germany, www.clipland.com/corporate, contact@clipland.com.
Cover art based on C64 by Luca Boldrini, CC-BY.

BISAC book classifications:

COM052000 COMPUTERS / Reference
COM043000 COMPUTERS / Networking / General
COM034000 COMPUTERS / Interactive & Multimedia

Cataloging Data:

Title:	Micropolis BBS Primer
Author:	Micropolis Handbooks
Publisher:	Micropolis Press
ISBN:	978-3-9826166-1-2
pages:	92
cm:	4.9 mm (0.19in) spine; 216m x 140mm (8.5in x 5.5in)

Disclaimer

The information contained within this book is for educational and entertainment purposes only. Although every precaution has been taken in the preparation of this book, the author and the publisher ("we", "us", "Micropolis", "Clipland GmbH") assume no responsibility for errors or omissions. No warranties of any kind are expressed or implied. The reader agrees that we, under no circumstances, are responsible for any losses, direct or indirect, which are incurred as a result of the use of information contained within this text. Changes are periodically made to the information herein; these changes will be incorporated in new editions of the publication. Readers acknowledge that we are not engaging in the rendering of legal, financial, medical, technical or professional advice. For more information, the author and publisher may be contacted at the previously stated address.

MICROPOLIS PROVIDES THIS PUBLICATION "AS IS" WITHOUT WARRANTY OF ANY KIND, EITHER EXPRESS OR IMPLIED, INCLUDING, BUT NOT LIMITED TO, THE IMPLIED WARRANTIES OF NON-INFRINGEMENT, MERCHANTABILITY OR FITNESS FOR A PARTICULAR PURPOSE. Some jurisdictions do not allow disclaimer of express or implied warranties in certain transactions, therefore, this statement may not apply to you.

Statements regarding Micropolis' future direction or intent are subject to change or withdrawal without notice, and represent goals and objectives only.

Trademarks

Many of the designations used by manufacturers and sellers to distinguish their products or services are claimed as trademarks. Where those designations appear in this text and Micropolis and/or the authors were aware of a trademark claim, the designations are mentioned along with their owners and may be additionally marked with a trademark symbol. Their use here within this text is for educational use of the reader and is covered under nominative fair use. Micropolis is in no way suggesting support, sponsorship or endorsement of the owner of these trademarks. Only as much of such marks is used as is necessary to identify the trademark owner, product, or service.

Links

This publication provides links to external content as a convenience and for informational purposes only; they do not constitute an endorsement, support, sponsorship or an approval by us. We bear no responsibility for the accuracy, legality or content of the external site or for that of subsequent links.

Comments welcome

We want our Micropolis Handbooks series of publications to be as helpful as possible. If you encounter errors, omissions or would like to share your comments about this book with us, feel free to contact Micropolis via email or the form found at:

https://www.micropolis.com/contact

Table of Contents

Introduction

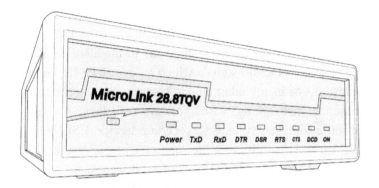

This text, based in structure on a frequently asked questions (FAQ) document, is a collection of short articles aiming to help you with a quick-start on the topic of Bulletin Board Systems, so called BBS. We here explain common terms that were the computer lingo of 1980s dial-up and BBS users and try shed light on some of the technologies involved in operating or calling a BBS in the olden days of computers. Surprisingly, in a renaissance of BBS in the wake of retro computing, these things are still relevant today and we hope to preserve some of the reality or even mindset of what it was like to go on-line back then through documenting how it all worked.

What is Dial-up

Historically, users would "call Boards", that meant using facilities of the public switched telephone network (PSTN) to establish a connection to a remote computer system running a bulletin board software. This was "calling a BBS via dial-up line". And the available lines of a BBS were usually called "nodes". Such a link is a one-to-one or point-to-point channel where communication is secured via the privacy guaranteed by the PSTN infrastructure and by laws such as the US American Convention on Human Rights Article 11's "Right to Privacy" or European legislation like the "Fernmeldegeheimnis". Users would use devices called a "modem" to modulate digital data "sentences" as audio signals which a normal PSTN line could transmit - as in any other human conversation via phone. Early computer networking wasn't "always on". People would call specific computer systems for a certain service. USENET was a dial-up service in its first incarnation. CompuServe in the US, BTX in Germany, Minitel in France all were dial-up. Bulletin Board Systems were dial-up. Some BBS offered gateways into larger networks, or offered exchange with messaging networks like FidoNet, FsxNet, RelayNet, WWIVnet, the USENET or the World Wide Web (WWW) commonly called "Internet" to-day. But all of this was dial-up and meant that a user was taxed a fee for each minute the computer was on-line.

What is a Modem

A "Modem", short for "modulator-demodulator", is a computer hardware device for the conversion of data from a digital for-mat into a format suitable for an analog transmission, usually with a BBS or Internet access this means transmission via a (PSTN) telephone line. This functionality is most obvious in early modems that were built as an "acoustic coupler", a device resembling a telephone handset, where a normal telephone handset could be coupled in - like matching two handsets re-versed, mirrored, so that each microphone was listening to the speaker, and each speaker talked into the microphone of the other handset. Only that with an acoustic coupler, a computer produced noises for transmission through the phone line that another computer on the other end could pick up, decipher and re-translate into digital information on the other end. A modem transmits data by producing special noises, a process that is actually the modulation of one or more carrier wave signals to encode digital information. A receiving modem "hears" the noises and demodulates the signal to recreate the original digital information. Modem users and dial-up enthusiasts are sometimes called "Modemers". Fax machines are also using modems internally and produce the same familiar noises upon connect.

In hobbyist or computer amateur contexts of the 1970s, 1980s and 1990s, digital data channels between computer systems were usually established over ordinary switched telephone lines that were not designed for data use. Audio quality was low and the signal to noise distance less than perfect. That meant that digital data, the modulated data, must work within these constraints, take the limited frequency spectrum of a normal voice audio signal into account and compensate for line defects. Early modems, including acoustically coupled modems, relied on the user (or on an additional device, an automatic calling unit) to actually dial and establish a voice connection before putting the handset into the acoustic coupler or switching a modem to line. Of course, this quickly improved and more modern modems were are able to perform the tedious actions needed to connect a call through a telephone exchange on their own. Also the "acoustic coupler" form vanished and was replaced by modems directly accepting the telephone connector plug (RJ11, "registered jack" or 4P4C) as the "speaker to microphone"-configuration was a source of more noise interference for a connection anyway. Modems since then were built in a form-factor of a VHS cassette and were able to pick up the line, to dial, could understand signals sent back by phone company equipment (dialtone, ringing, busy signal), could recognizing incoming ring signals and answer calls if configured to do so.

One milestone in modem technology was the Hayes Smartmodem, introduced in 1981. The Smartmodem was a 300 baud direct-connect modem, but its innovation was a command language which allowed the computer to make control requests, such as commands to dial or answer calls. A modem was connected to a computer via the RS-232 serial interface, either via a wide DB-25 connector, the smaller DE-9 D-Sub connector or smaller custom 9-pin connectors. The Hayes commands were then sent over the same connection as the data itself, made possible by two operating modes ("data" and "command mode") which could be switched by special escaped sequences and pauses in the serial data stream. The Hayes commands used by this device became a de-facto standard, the "Hayes command set", which was integrated into devices by many other manufacturers and, to this date, many incarnations of modems - even GSM cellular modems - use the Hayes command set.

Over the years, higher modem speeds became available, growing from 300 baud over 2.400, 9600 baud and 14.400 baud to many kilobaud. This came to an end when modems were able to exhaust the theoretically available bandwidth of a phone line at about 56 kbit/s. The used modulation schemes at that point were so sophisticated, that some schemes, despite standardization, were incompatible between manufactures and BBS SysOps often advertised which modem, model or make they were operating on which BBS node.

What is ISDN?

During the 1990s, an evolution of traditional PSTN phone lines reached end users in the form of ISDN, or Integrated Services Digital Network. The public phone system became increasingly digital and ISDN was the product that ambitious customers could lease in regions where it became available. The ISDN system offers two 64 kbit/s "bearer" lines and a single 16 kbit/s "delta" channel for commands and data. With dedicated ISDN cards, users could replace their modems and eliminate the "audio translation element" by directly switching to a data channel natively designed for digital transmission. An ISDN line could max out the available phone bandwidth while it maintained a more reliable and compatible connection than via modem. Each ISDN endpoint provided two voice/data channels of 64 kbit/s (or 56 kbit/s in some countries) that could be bundled for double speed and one always-on data channel for call signaling and/or basic always-on Internet access (if providers allowed). But as these improvements didn't matter much for an average consumer, ISDN saw relatively little uptake in the wider market and ISDN data transmission was quickly replaced by DSL or its most widely rolled out ADSL technology (asymmetric digital subscriber line). ADSL is what runs an always-on broadband Internet connection today, although it's quite surprising that hundred thousands of users worldwide still use dial-up and a modem to connect to the Internet today.

Probably one of the most exhaustive guides on modems, their use and technical details, was written by David S. Lawyer and can be found, for example, here [tldp.org/HOWTO/Modem-HOWTO.html]. More links to material about modems, BBS and all can be found at the end of this document in "Further reading and material elsewhere".

5

What are the meanings of the abbreviations and lights on the front-panel of my modem?

On the front panel of an analog modem, there are usually a number of LED lights, labeled with abbreviations that indicate various device conditions. Here is a listing. As a rule of thumb, the more lights light up, the more complete a connection is. For the actual meaning, please refer to the section "Connecting your modem" where some basics of RS-232 are outlined.

```
TxD - Data is being sent activity
      (sometimes just "TX")
RxD - Data is being received
      (sometimes just "RX")
DTR - Data Terminal Ready
DSR - Data Signal Ready
RTS - Ready to Send
CTS - Clear to Send
DCD - Data Carrier Ready
OH  - Off-Hook, the handset is off the
      hookswitch, well, with a modem
      not having a handset, it means
      the modem "picked up" or is "on
      line"
```

Old Hayes modems also used these abbreviations:

```
HS - High-speed (4,800 and above)
AA - Auto-answer
CD - Carrier detect
RD - Receive data (same as Rx)
SD - Send data (same as Tx)
TR - Terminal ready (same as CTS?)
MR - Modem ready (same as DTR?)
VO - Voice
RI - Ring Indicator
```

How can I dial into a BBS in 2023?

There's a renaissance of Bulletin Board Systems going on worldwide and retro computer enthusiasts old and young are using different means to connect to BBS. Many of these new old-skool "Boards" are reachable via Telnet and some even via dial-up phone line.

via in-browser Telnet

Connecting to a BBS via Telnet is probably the easiest way to explore the hidden realms of Bulletin Board Systems. You can opt for an in-browser Telnet emulator, use a terminal emulator on the command line or fire up an all-in-one communicator package with built-in dialer, phonebook and terminal emulation.

via Modem

Traditionally, you would connect to a BBS via the public phone system, using a modem. This document here has pointers on how to connect a modem to your computer, how terminals work and how you can get them working nowadays. And you can find links to directories of active BBS that still offer dial-up nodes. One thing to point out it that the transition to an all-digital IP-based telephone infrastructure (Voice over IP, VOIP) may interfere with how modems work and modems may fail in setting up a connection. Read the section "Using an analog modem over a Voice-over-IP line" for additional help with that.

via Modem-Emulation (which is actually TCP/IP Telnet)

Many retro home computers, like the C64, have all it needs to control a modem and dial into BBS. But users may not want to actually block a land-line or they might want to connect to a BBS that doesn't offer dial-up nodes. On the other hand, many retro computers have no means of talking Telnet over TCP/IP. For this scenario there's a nifty adapter called "WiFi232" or "WiModem232". It connects to your computer and emulates a Hayes compatible modem for your system. Your computer is then able to talk to this modem serially, like it was a real modem, only the AT command to dial a number is slightly different. Instead of a phone number, you specify an IP address or domain name plus optional Telnet port. The modem emulator then initiates a TCP/IP connection to this system. The emulator itself is logged into your wireless LAN WiFi network and has full Internet access. It works like a Modem-Telnet bridge for your older computer system.

What is Baud

Baud (abbreviated as "Bd", named after Emile Baudot) is the unit used to measure the symbol rate of a transmission over a data channel. It describes the frequency changes of a signal (or "status changes", "transitions", or "steps") on a transmission channel per second. 1 Baud equals one step per second. It is not the same as bits per second ("bits/s" or "bps") but is very often used interchangeably. Baud means how many symbols per second are transmitted, where each symbol is one step. Each symbol now, depending on the modulation scheme in use, usually encodes four, eight or more bits in each signal change. That's why the bps rate of a transmission is usually higher than the

Baud rate. V.32 uses a step rate of 2400 Baud and transmits at a rate of 9600 bps. A different scheme sends 6 bits per symbol at 2400 Baud for 14400 bps.

The fact that a modem's speed is usually given in bps isn't only due to marketing exploiting the higher number to advertise a product, but has the same historic reason why people tend to use Baud and bps interchangeably. Early modems encoded one bit in one phase change, thus, bps and Baud number would be the same and were both used to describe the effective bit rate, or "speed", of a modem. When new modem communication standards arrived, the effective bit rate started to exceed the Baud rate and confusion entailed.

One more detail worth noting is, that there's usually a difference in data rate between modems (modem-to-modem) and rates used on the serial connection cable between your computer and your modem (computer-to-modem). The first, the "DCE" rate is the speed a modem uses for communications over a common telephone line and is usually given in bps. The abbreviation "DCE" is short for "Data Communications Equipment", which means "your modem". The other abbreviation, "DTE", is short for "Data Terminal Equipment" and is used to indicate your computer (or terminal), the device your modem is connected to. It is also given in bps and on these local serial lines Baud rate and Symbol rate are usually the same. Knowing about this difference, DTE and DCE, you should actually speak of DCE Baud rate of a modem when the rate between modems is   meant.

Probably one of the most exhaustive guides on modems, their use and technical details was written by David S. Lawyer and can be found, for example, here [tldp.org/HOWTO/Modem-HOWTO.html].

What is a Terminal?

A computer terminal is an electronic (or even electromechanical device) that is used for entering data into or transcribing data coming from a computer system. Most common are character-oriented terminals, where the terminal displays entered ("echoes") or received characters on screen (historically on paper). A user either writes text strings on a prompt line or the system outputs lines of text, one character at a time. Usually 80 characters per line - as this is how many chars would fit in one line on a piece of office paper. Ultimately a line is completed with a "carriage return" and "line feed". This way the output or displayed text is scrolled, so that only the last several lines (typically 24) are visible (80x25 characters). It depends on the terminal implementation (or today on its mode of operation) if a text string will be buffered until the ENTER key is pressed, so the application receives a ready string of text, or if each character is transmitted right after input.

One of the early electronic terminals, the DEC VT100, was one of the first terminals to support special "escape sequences" or "escape codes" for cursor control, text line manipulation and manipulation of the keyboard status, lights etc. This scheme for "escape codes" started the de-facto standard for hardware video terminals and later terminal emulators that led to the "ANSI X3.64" standard for terminals. In MS DOS these escape codes are usable through the ANSI.SYS driver which helps emulate an "ANSI terminal" and further contributed to the widespread use of the term "ANSI" for an "extended ASCII" character set with optional "escape sequences" to control the cursor or color specific parts of the output.

Note that a terminal or terminal emulator is not Telnet. A terminal receives, processes and displays serial data according to the

10

ANSI terminal specs. It won't understand or process Telnet's "interpret as command" sequences or the various other Telnet specific terminal extensions. But terminal emulators usually can run telnet as a layer between a remote system and their display, running telnet "in fullscreen mode", where telnet then feeds "serial ANSI data" to the actual terminal display.

As with many de-facto standards, the problem here is that there are many different terminals and terminal emulators, each with its own set of escape sequences or capabilities. Special libraries (such as curses) have been created, together with terminal description databases, such as Termcap and Terminfo, to help unify "talking" to different terminals - but to this date, especially with color, the actual displayed output of a specific escape sequence can't be really predicted and even depends on user settings or activated desktop themes. Referring to the example of text coloring, there is no strict definition of a specific color. Although the "ANSI standard" defines basic colors by name, systems and users may define which shade of red, blue, green, etc. the application actually outputs. Further, the ANSI escape codes for "bold" text display are commonly used to add 8 more shades to the basic 8 colors intended, but as this as well is just a suggestion, it can't be expected that "bold red" actually outputs "bright red" and not just "a red character in bold" - or some completely unrelated shade of color. The aixterm specification tried to overcome at least this ambiguous coloring but is an equally unbinding suggestion.

Later terminals started offering the ability to alter colors by accepting longer escape sequences, with more numerical values indicating more shades of colors, but implementation differences here again resulted in not 100% predictable color renditions. Today's terminal emulators, like Xterm, Ubuntu's terminal, GNOME Terminal, KDE's Konsole, iTerm and libvte based terminals allow "true color" 24-bit colors with a triplet RGB escape sequence resembling rgb or hex color in HTML.

One historical note is that electromechanical devices called a "teleprinter" (or "teletypewriter", "teletype" or "TTY") were used for telegraphy and later more generic typed text transmission. Developed in the late 1830s and 1840s they saw more widespread use in the late 1880s. Such machines were decades later adapted to provide a user interface to early mainframe computers and minicomputers, sending typed data to the computer and printing the response. Today's computer systems still use the term "TTY" in reminiscence of these machines, calling "virtual console" or "virtual terminal", the user interface of a computer system, a "tty".

One anecdote in relation to early terminals is that many computer hobbyists converted an IBM Selectric electric typewriter into a computer terminal, basically by adding a RS-232 serial interface to it. This was possible as the Selectric had a unique printing mechanism featuring a ball with 44 character stamps on it. Using a clever mechanism called a "whiffletree" digital input was converted to analog ball steering motions (effectively a simple Digital to Analog converter, DAC). Converting an IBM Selectric was a relatively inexpensive and fairly popular way of getting a printing computer terminal during the years of the late 1960s and throughout the 1970s. The machine produced high quality hard-copy computer output and could be driven at its optimum and relatively high data-rate of 134.5 baud. The Selectric conversion terminals were so popular that computer manufacturers even started supporting this 134.5 baud data rate instead of the more common 110 baud.

Detecting your terminal type

As the example of terminal text color has shown, not all terminals behave consistently. This led to the development of the terminfo database (formerly named termcap, for terminal capabilities) and the introduction of the "tput" command. On Linux, tput is available from the ncurses package and is the frontend of the terminfo database found in /usr/share/terminfo/. This database is a library of the vast number of terminals that can be found in the wild and curates their capabilities and escape code sequences used for a fixed set of common terminal operations. All these terminal commands are then exposed through a fixed vocabulary of commands, the terminfo API, and can be accessed through tput. For example, if you want to write your own program that does specific terminal operations, for example sending the cursor to the home position in the top left corner of the display, you don't have to do terminal detection on your own or find specific ANSI escape codes to do it for different terminals, but instead you use tput. tput will read the terminal type your're currently using from the $TERM environment variable, look-up the sequence for "go home" from the terminfo database and output it to STDOUT for you (thus "tput"). For example. Try

```
$ echo $TERM
```

to see what your terminal would tell tput about itself. Then try

```
$ tput home
```

.

This terminal detection works locally, but it doesn't via Telnet or won't work in sessions with remote BBS. The $TERM variable isn't transmitted as part of some standardized "Telnet handshake". This shortcoming is in parts remedied by a Telnet command called TTYPE, which a proper Telnet implementation will answer with a string similar to the $TERM environment variable value. But as so often with Telnet and terminals, this is a moving target. For example, the well-known terminal hyperterm on Windows (and its built-in Telnet implementation) will identify itself as "ANSI" by default. Try feeding this to tput via the -T switch and tput will tell you that it doesn't know a terminal named "ANSI". Also, BBS type serial communication often happened in the early days of computing and connecting to a BBS usually meant that people using an IBM compatible PC would connect to "DOS BBS", while people with Ataris would call Boards for Atari owners or Commodore users would call Commodore BBS and so forth. With these closed circles it was quite safe to assume a specific set of capabilities on the other end of the (dial-up) line. Also, these connections usually didn't include a Telnet client in the communication chain (compare the notes about a terminal emulator not being Telnet in this document). Detecting the type of remote terminal mattered more in professional use scenarios or in today's renaissance of BBS where people might call a BBS via Telnet, via Dial-up, with a Windows PC, a Mac, from a Linux box or with their choice of beloved retro computer running an ancient version of some ancient terminal emulator. That's why many BBS in the olden days but also to this date do a Q&A session about the terminal in use with their visitors upon connect.

What is Telnet?

Telnet is an old protocol to transmit keystrokes from your keyboard to a remote system and receive on-screen feedback, text and simple graphics, on your local screen as if you would sit in front of the remote system on its console. Telnet is one of the first Internet standards and its name is commonly translated as being the abbreviation of "teletype network". Telnet is a simple protocol layer which may operate on a serial data link, like a RS232 serial line, where data Bytes are modulated as electrical signals and are transmitted with a certain speed (Baud rate) or Telnet may operate over more sophisticated network means like the 1970s / 1980s Network Control Protocol (NCP) or today's TCP/IP protocol stack, which has long replaced NCP. The Telnet endpoint of a remote system is usually reachable under the remote system's IP or domain address on port 23.

Note that Telnet and "a terminal" isn't the same thing. Telnet is an element or "layer" that is usually in-between a terminal or terminal emulator and a remote system. Telnet clients are capable of responding to so-called "interpret as command" (IAC) byte sequences and change their behavior accordingly. A terminal doesn't use or understand these IAC sequences. So Telnet extends what a terminal can do. As a gateway element in a communication data stream, Telnet then outputs a "serial ANSI X3.64 conforming" data stream to a connected terminal, or the terminal emulator it is running in, usually in "full screen" mode, and the terminal emulator will display this data.

Telnet is an unencrypted clear text protocol. Historically, it was assumed that the "line" you are communicating over is private by design, for example a dedicated phone line, twisted copper wire, an analog PSTN line or later a digital ISDN channel. These technologies didn't require an encrypted envelope. But when Telnet communication began to migrate towards the Internet and public IP networks, the need for encryption arose and Telnet was superseded by SSH (Secure Shell Protocol) which, in essence, is still Telnet but uses elaborate mechanisms for a safe encrypted handshake upon initial connection and then communicates via completely encrypted packets over the transport channel, usually on port 22.

Some BBSs offer Telnet on different ports than 23. This is mostly to make it a bit harder for abusive connects from bots and similar agents to probe such a well-known port or stems from the fact that ports on a system below 1024 require elevated user privileges to be opened and thus expose the process offering the service to greater threats.

What are Telnet commands?

Over Telnet, all data octets except 0xff are transmitted as is. There are three common numeral systems (or notations) to describe Byte values in computing: hexadecimal, decimal and octal. The hexadecimal byte "0xff", or "255" in decimal and "377" in octal notation is the highest value an 8-bit byte can represent and in Telnet, it is called the "IAC byte", IAC for "Interpret As Command". This byte signals that the next byte is a telnet command. The command to insert 0xff into the stream is 0xff, so 0xff must be escaped by doubling it when sending data over the telnet protocol.

Note that "ANSI escape codes" are a different thing from "Telnet commands". Telnet commands communicate with the terminal *itself* while ANSI escape codes control the presentation of content *within* a terminal. Refer to the section on Terminals and ANSI escape codes for an explanation of the latter.

Telnet is described in RFC854 [datatracker.ietf.org/doc/html/rfc854] and this RFC also details how IAC work (on page 13 of the RFC): "All Telnet commands consist of at least a two byte sequence: the 'Interpret as Command' (IAC) escape character followed by the code for the command. The commands dealing with option negotiation are three byte sequences, the third byte being the code for the option referenced. This format was chosen so that a more comprehensive use of the "data space" is made, (...) collisions of data bytes with reserved command values will be minimized, all such collisions requiring the inconvenience, and inefficiency, of 'escaping' the data bytes into the stream. With the current set-up, only the IAC need be doubled to be sent as data, and the other 255 codes may be passed transparently."

The following are the defined TELNET commands. Note that these codes and code sequences have the indicated meaning only when immediately preceded by an IAC.

Command NAME	Decimal CODE	Code MEANING
SE	240	End of subne-gotiation para-meters.
NOP	241	No operation.
Data Mark	242	The data stream portion of a Sync. This should always be accom-panied by a TCP Urgent notificat-tion.
Break	243	NVT character BRK.
Interrupt Process	244	The function IP.
Abort output	245	The function AO.
Are You There	246	The function AYT.
Erase character	247	The function EC.
Erase Line	248	The function EL.
Go ahead	249	The GA signal.

SB	250	Indicates that what follows is subnegotiation of the indi cated option.
WILL (option code)	251	Indicates the desire to begin performing, or confirmation that you are now per- forming, the indi- cated option.
WON'T (option code)	252	Indicates the refusal to per- form, or continue performing, the indicated option.
DO (option code)	253	Indicates the re- quest that the other party per- form, or confir- mation that you are expecting the other party to perform, the indicated option.
DON'T (option code)	254	Indicates the de- mand that the other party stop perfor- ming, or confir- mation that you are no longer ex- expecting the other party to perform, the indicated option.
IAC	255	Data Byte 255.

A Telnet client and server may negotiate options using telnet commands at any stage during the connection. There are well over 40 Telnet options that were specified in various RFCs over the years but in practice, only a dozen codes are commonly used:

| Decimal | Name of | RFC defining |
| CODE | the option | the option |
	NAME	RFC
0	Transmit Binary	856
1	Echo	857
3	Suppress Go Ahead	858
5	Status	859
6	Timing Mark	860
24	Terminal Type	1091
31	Window Size	1073
32	Terminal Speed	1079
33	Remote Flow Control	1372
34	Linemode	1184
36	Environment Variables	1408

Is there a secure Telnet?

So, Telnet is a "cleartext" protocol, without any means to encrypt its sent data. But hey, Telnet is only one layer of the communication channel - wouldn't it be possible to send Telnet over a secure channel of sorts? Well, yes, and there are in essence two ways to make Telnet a secure way of communicating:

The most obvious way of securing a Telnet communication is by sending it over a channel that is per-se secure. A land-line dial-up line, where Telnet is used to establish a one-to-one channel inside a medium that is secured by telecommunication standards is secure Telnet. Or by using Telnet on a private network or via a virtual private network. That makes it secure as well. So, if you tunnel Telnet through an encrypted channel, Telnet can be secure - but remember that Telnet on its own isn't secure.

What is TelnetS?

Yes, you read that right, it's Telnet - with an "S" at the end, and it doesn't mean the plural of Telnet. There is a not so well known "standard" for a secured version of Telnet, and its name is "TelnetS". We here wrote the last letter as a capital, to differentiate it from the plural form of the word. Similarly as with the two versions of a "secure FTP", there's a name variant for Telnet (FTPS is FTP over TLS/SSL, and SFTP a synonym for the SSH2 File Transfer Protocol, another example is HTTP and HTTPS), and a suffixed "S" indicates that *TelnetS* is Telnet over TLS/SSL (Secure Socket Layer).

TelnetS is enabled by a modified telnet daemon, telnetd, which is available on Debian systems via the package *telnetd-ssl*. The SSL telnetd daemon replaces normal telnetd and adds SSL authentication and encryption. It inter-operates with normal telnetd in both directions. It checks if the other side is also talking SSL, if not it falls back to normal telnet protocol. If this hasn't become clear yet: this means passwords and data sent will not go in cleartext over the line. It has been agreed that secure *telnetd* listens for incoming connections on port 992. The bad news in regards to this "secure Telnet" is the fact that it is not well supported and known. This might be due to the unfortunate naming or the alternative of SSH. Outside from IBM, where TelnetS was suggested as a secure alternative for some systems, you won't really find it in the wild.

Note that a server talking TelnetS does also require your client to be TelnetS enabled. A telnet executable with SSL support compiled in might provide the "-z" switch, where you can say you want SSL encryption ("-z SSL"). Such a telnet client can come in handy to debug HTTPS connections when connecting to port 443 with it. One other note is that TelnetS is not the same as using a command that is able to establish an arbitrary network connection, like netcat or openssl. While you may use a command like "openssl s_client -host example.com -port 992" to connect to a SSL encrypted endpoint, openssl won't be able to really "speak" Telnet. That's because TelnetS, just like Telnet, in parts uses special binary escape sequences which openssl won't understand. These binary sequences are explained above in "What are Telnet commands?". In short, telnet uses the IAC (interpret as command) byte (value 255, hex FF) to start a command sequence. If this byte is sent as data, then it must be "escaped" by prepending it with another value 255/hex FF (that means on the wire: "IAC IAC", "255 255", "FF FF"). Not "knowing" about this protocol convention and not obeying this standard means the data stream will become corrupted once the remote Telnet server starts to negotiate protocol specific things.

What Terminal emulators can I use?

Note that some terminal emulators are just that, a terminal emulator. While other programs are communication suites, which are made of a component to talk to modems via serial line or other connections, a phone book or address database to manage your collection of BBS or Telnet servers to connect to, logging and tracing means to record sessions with remote Boards and finally a terminal emulator that will handle the actual connection, sometimes with optional SSH support, and software extensions to handle in-band or out-of-band file uploads or file downloads via popular binary data transfer protocols like KERMIT, YMODEM, XMODEM or ZMODEM and their variants.

At this point you may have understood that a terminal or terminal emulator is more like a "window", or "browser", it is how you "look" at a data stream, but how this data stream arrives at your system is another story. Telnet is one way, or a directly connected socket another, it may also be via a device that presents itself as a serial port. Terminals may have built in means to bring data to your "window" via a dial-up line with integrated phonebook in a communication suite designed for modem communication, or it may be be brought in via a package that has built-in Telnet, SSH, or all of those means. But a terminal on its own might also be very bare-bones - and this in turn might suffice for serial connections, like common in talking to development boards, like Arduino or ESP8266. Examples of bare-bones "only a terminal" applications are gtkterm and the very excellent for serial line debugging HTerm [www.der-hammer.info/pages/terminal.html].

On Linux / *nix

On *nix systems there is a selection of terminal programs available, usually called "the console". xterm, rxvt, GNOME Terminal, and Konsole These terminals and command consoles usually support at least a portion of ANSI escape code sequences to control your display, text and cursor layout. Terminal emulators are typically used to interact with a Unix shell locally on a machine. To access a remote system there needs to be a bridge in-between that communicates via network with this remote system. In early computing, this tool was the unencrypted Telnet protocol, implemented in the similarly named *telnet* program executable. So in order to "dial" into a BBS, which in essence is accessing a remote system via terminal emulator, you would use Telnet inside your terminal emulator to go online. the telnet command will then act as a "full screen" application inside your terminal emulator. The telnet command is probably the first option anyone would chose, but the very handy *screen* program can also be run in "telnet mode".

- Linux telnet command in your terminal of choice

- Linux "screen" in Telnet mode

Few people know that the popular *screen* terminal emulator and multiplexer is able to operate in "Telnet mode" when it was compiled with the ENABLE_TELNET option defined (which is usually the case). Start screen like so:

```
$ screen //telnet 127.0.0.1 23
```

to connect to local host in telnet mode at port 23. You see, when the first option to screen is "//telnet", it expects a host and port as 2nd and 3rd parameter. Refer to the screen man page for further help, but usage is generally straightforward.

For BBS SysOps it might be interesting to note that screen in Telnet mode will identify itself with the name "screen" in response to a TTYPE request, unless instructed otherwise.

- PuTTY - stand-alone software implemented terminal emulator and telnet communication program.

- Qodem (under wine) - an excellent terminal and communication suite. It emulates a number of terminals faithfully, has an integrated phonebook best in class features like reliable session capturing and renders fonts like few others. Even on Linux under wine it perform flawlessly and once you get the 'all keyboard shortcuts' interface, it is a joy to use.

- Tera Term (under wine, see below) - despite some rough edges in terms of font configuration and color interpretation a solid terminal.

- HyperTerminal (under wine, see below)

- Netrunner

- SyncTERM

- kermit

- uxterm, rxvt, xterm, urxvt, dtterm - there are many terminals more on *nix systems

cu - very simple terminal with dial-in functionality ("cu" is short for "call up")

tip - very simple terminal from the early days to connect to remote systems, also with dial-in and socket connect functionality

On Windows / DOS

IBM PC clones had an 80×25 character display mode with 16 colors and special graphics characters. This was known as ANSI or more precisely the IBM "OEM font" CP437 with support for ANSI color (escape codes, as interpreted by ANSI.SYS). Despite that, DOS and Windows didn't really come with a default terminal client. That said, there are a number of good options available - although the Windows-bundled Hyper-term isn't necessarily the best option.

PuTTy - mature cross-platform terminal. On PC, though, it is usually set to the wrong charset by default. So go into preferences, and there into "Translation". Look for option "Remote character set" and change iso8859-1 to UTF-8 to have putty munge utf-8 encoded cp437 block characters etc.

Hyperterminal

On DOS/ Windows up to roughly Windows XP Professional, the system came with a default terminal emulator called "hyperterminal" or hypertrm.exe on the filesystem. It didn't ship with Windows 7/8/10. In order to run hyperterminal you only need two files, a file called hypertrm.dll and the executable hypertrm.exe. You should commonly find hypertrm.exe in C:\Program Files\Windows NT and hypertrm.dll in C:\Windows\System32. If you can't find it on your system or you are running a Linux box but would like to use hyperterminal under wine (which works), then you can get hold of an "Installation" or "System Builder" CDROM and extract the two files from there.

On the Windows XP CD, both of these files are in the i386 directory. Copy them over and while you're at it copying hypertrm.chm and hypertrm.hlp with them wouldn't hurt. As you might notice, the file suffixes are not .exe or .dll but all files on the installation medium end in a dash, "hypertrm.ex_" and "hypertrm.dl_". These files are archived, compressed so called .CAB (Cabinet) files, an archive format used by Microsoft. It can be easily extracted/inflated with common archiving utilities, like the Ubuntu "built-in" file-roller. On Windows all compression utilities should do the job as well, even the Explorer built-in one, if you select both files, right-click on any of the high-lighted files and click on "Extract".

Like any other terminal emulator out there, hyperterminal implements cursor and display behavior in response to terminal escape sequences (ANSI escape codes), so character-mode full-screen applications (one example would be the lynx browser, or, obviously telnet) can run in hyperterminal's terminal window. Telnet is built into HyperTerm.

If you don't just start it up but go into hyperterminal's settings, you can choose from a set of built-in terminal configurations so hyperterminal emulates specific terminal types. And here come the problem: neither of them is implemented correctly. The one named "VT100" works so la la but does not pass extended characters commonly used for basic graphics. The config called "ANSIW" at least allows 8-bit ASCII mode and interprets ANSI color codes, but cp437 graphic chars end up garbled. Also most other things like default line terminator etc. are wrong and need be changed.

Once you are connected to some Telnet system, go to "File" > "properties" to change settings for the current connection. On the pop-up switch to the second tab for "Settings". "Emulation:" should be "ANSIW". "Telnet-" may say "ANSI" or "VT100", or whatever you had set before - it's the string HyperTerminal sends in response to a TTYPE (code 24) ANSI control code request by a remote system. Setting it to ANSI should be safe, so the other side doesn't expect xterm or even xterm-256colors capabilities but Hypertrm should be able to receive ANSI color codes. Now click on the button on the lower right, "ASCII Setup". In the upper options for "ASCII Sending" check both boxes, the checkbox for "send line ends with line feeds" and "Echo (typed characters locally)". In the lower area for "ASCII

26

Receiving" do not check "Append line feeds to incoming line ends" and do not check "Force incoming data to 7-bit ASCII", but you may check "break too long lines". If you see very strange glyphs instead of legible characters on display, try opening "View" and there "Change font". Select a different font and the displayed text should be readable normally. Once you have all those things in place, you should get half-baked terminal emulation with hypertrm.exe for basic Telnet, but expect newlines still be messed up.

Contrary to common belief, HyperTerminal wasn't written by Microsoft but by Hilgraeve, a Detroit/Michigan company, for Microsoft as a subcontractor. And the version shipped with Microsoft Windows is, well, let's say an "early version". The company continued to improve the software on its own and continues to sell it on their website as HyperTerminal PE [www.hilgraeve.com/hyperterminal/] (where "PE" is for "private edition") and their most up to date version, "HyperACCESS".

If you're adventurous and want to run the original Windows binary under Linux within wine emulator, you can do so. It works. Just don't use the initial "connection pop-up" that comes up once you open the program, but close it and go to "Call" to trigger a new connection pop-up. Otherwise wine will crash. Enter some name in the "New connection" pop-up line and click "OK". A next pop-up comes up and there you can select "Connect via:" > "TCP/IP (Winsock)" from a drop down selector, instead of the pre-selected serial port "COM1". Once you select "TCP/IP (Winsock)" you are offered different inputs for "Host address" and "Port number", the latter pre-populated with Telnet's common port 23. Once you're connected, make sure to change settings for terminal emulation like described above.

Tera Term

Tera Term (alternatively TeraTerm) is an open-source, free, software implemented, terminal emulator program from Japan. It emulates different types of computer terminals, from DEC VT100 to DEC VT382 and can be run on DOS/Windows or under wine emulation on Linux.

It has its own Wikipedia page [en.wikipedia.org/wiki/Tera_Term] and can be downloaded from ttssh2.osdn.jp [ttssh2.osdn.jp/] or www.teraterm.org as both domains point to the same server.

Setup can be a bit tricky. So once you've extracted the zip archive, locate the main binary ttermpro.exe. Don't try editing the shipped TERATERM.INI file as it's difficult to understand. Instead use the GUI of the program itself - it does the same. So, upon start, a "new connection" dialog comes up. Enter a server or IP for "Host" and "TCP port #" number. Select "Service": "Telnet" as Tera Term starts expecting an SSH connection. Usually, the first terminal output after "Connect" should be all gibberish, as the program is from Japan and the default settings expect Japanese ideograms. Go to "Setup" > "Font" > "Font..." and in the opened dialog select some western font you like and click "OK" - text should now be legible, refreshed without a reconnect. Then go to "Setup" > "Terminal..." and check "Local echo", and while you're on this dialog, enter "american" for "locale".

- Telix (often shipped with ELSA modems)

On Commodore 64

The Commodore 64 ("breadbin") has a native resolution of 40 by 25 characters. This comes from the hardware text mode of the VIC-II video chip the C64 uses. The built-in character set uses 8 bytes (for 8×8 pixels) for each of the 256 characters. These hardware capabilities mean that an 80 column mode (like on a VT100 ASCII terminal or an IBM PC-compatible emulating one) can only be implemented in software, and on the C64 this means using "bitmap mode". In "bitmap mode" the C64 exhibits a native resolution of 320 by 200 pixels. If one wants to display 80 chars per line in this mode, it means a screen budget of 4×8 pixels per character. Given that there needs to be a one-pixel gap between characters to be legible, characters can effectively only be 3 pixels wide.

- CCGMS [commodore.software/downloads/category/59-ccgms] - Terminal for the C64 with many extended and modded versions available

Handy Term [commodore.software/downloads/category/63-handy-term] - another C64 terminal and communication suite

- GGLabs Terminal [www.vintageisthenewold.com/gglabs-terminal-a-vt100-terminal-emulator-for-the-commodore-64] - a VT100 terminal emulator, monochrome display, with a custom software 80 columns display and support for serial speeds up to 115200 bauds

- CGTerm - while technically not a Terminal on the C64, this terminal emulates how connecting to Commodore BBS would look on native hardware, only cross platform.

On Commodore AMIGA

The Amiga with its 320×200 @ 60Hz (NTSC) and 320×256 @ 50Hz (PAL) display resolution is usually capable of displaying 80 columns wide terminal screens (like the C64). But as the Amiga is somewhere between the olden days and newer systems, some terminal programs can be toggled between 80 and 40 column modes.

Most terminals are available from aminet [aminet.net/]. A video tutorial on how to "dial" from an Amiga to Telnet via an USB telnet bridge is here [www.youtube.com/watch?v=aOOE7KrrCpE].

- 64Door

- ColorTerm

- A-Talk III by Felsina Software in 1986, Published by OXXI

Amtelnet, DCTelnet, virterm, AmTelnet-II, Term

On Commodore PET

The very early hardware of the COmmodore PET makes connecting to a BBS a DIY adventure, but it is doable, as described here [biosrhythm.com/?p=1359]. - McTERM - released in 1980 by Madison Computer from Madison, WI, USA, manuals here [mikenaberezny.com/hardware/pet-cbm/madison-computer-mcterm/]. - PET-TERM - on github [github.com/ChartreuseK/PETTERM]

- Terminal v11 (listing [archive.org/details/transactor-magazines-v3-i06] in Transactor Magazine)

On Atari ST/STE/MEGA/TT/Falcon

Note that with the Atari ST emulator "Hatari" it is possible to run a terminal program on an emulated Atari and "dial" into modern BBS via Telnet.

- Connect 95 [sites.google.com/site/stessential/communications/connect] - released 1992 by Lars & Wolfgang Wander, Shareware

- FLASH [sites.google.com/site/stessential/communications/flash-vt100] - released 1986 by Joe Chiazzese & Alan page, VT100 emulation with ZMODEM integration

- TAZ [sites.google.com/site/stessential/communications/taz] - released 1994 by Neat n Nifty, able to do ANSI 16 Color

- ANSITerm - by Timothy Miller, released by Two World Software, only term able to display PC-like 16 color ANSI emulation with the help of a custom 3 pixel wide font and running in low resolution mode

- NeoCom [sites.google.com/site/stessential/communications/neocom] - Shareware, ASCII/VT52/ANSI Emulation

- Freeze Dried Terminal (FzDT)

- BobTerm - 40 columns and only up to 300 baud

- VanTerm

On Apple / Macintosh

On Apple systems, terminals usually only look good after installing and using a font that has old-style block characters as required by the CP437 charset. Look for a font named "Andale

Mono", which has these chars. Also note that Apple terminals tend to skew the CGA color scheme into a bleached realm. If you want to make sure that ANSI art looks as originally intended, you can invest the time to configure your colors along the original CGA specification [en.wikipedia.org/wiki/ Color_Graphics_Adapter#Color_palette].

iTerm/iTerm2 - set a proper font like Andale Mono in "Preferences" > "Profiles", tab "Text".

Terminal.app - define a custom profile in "Preferences" > profile "Pro" and set "Andale Mono" as font; also set "use bright colors for bold text".

On MSX

- BadCat terminal (by Andres Ortiz, load via bdterm.bin, 80 cols mode via bdshell)

Connecting your modem

Here we'll discuss how to connect your modem to set things up. First, some notes on how to connect your modem to the phone line and then notes on how to connect your modem to your computer, the different options with serial and USB and how to debug your terminal setup.

Connecting your modem to the phone line

The telephone line the modem is connected to must provide loop disconnect signaling (pulse dialing) or DTMF signaling (tone dialing). Tone dialing is by far the most used method world wide and your phone line usually is of the tone dial type. The modem is connected via standard modular telephone jack, type RJ11.

Within private branch exchange (PABX), dialing an external number may require the user to insert a PSTN access digit, e.g. a digit 9 (external access code). PBX systems are known from larger office installations but are also common in private homes.

A telephone line uses direct current and alternating current for ring signals. The telephone line circuit (TNV) can have hazardous voltage and must not be touched. On some modems, there are two RJ45 jacks (rectangular connectors, accepting usually clear plastic plugs), one connector for "PHONE" and another for "LINE". In case your modem has only one connector, make sure you use the correct line cable between your modem and the wall outlet - there might be differences in how lines are connected through.

In parts of Europe, Germany, Luxembourg an Liechtenstein, a wall connector named TAE-connector is used (in Austria, the similar shaped TDO-connector). There are different plugs, with different contact plates for TAE connector type "F" (for telephones, "Fernsprechgerät" in German) and type "N" (for other devices such as answering machines and modems, German "Nebengerät" or "Nebenstelle"). If your modem is plugged into the wall outlet with a cable suitable for type "F" it will get incoming ring signals, but it won't be able to switch to line and will not work! You must use a cable with an "N"-type wall connector and an RJ45 plug on the other end to plug into your modem. Getting a RING signal on incoming calls on terminal does not mean the line is correctly connected! Also note that once you plug a TAE "N" plug into the wall outlet you break the circuit for the "F" connector - so the other end RJ45 plug must be plugged into the "N" device (your modem) as well or the phone connected to the "F"-connector won't work anymore. Background is that the "N"-sockets on a TAE socket form a daisy-chain. Your provider's network service lines enter the socket and connect to pins 1 and 2 on the right-most "N"-connector. From there, service is daisy-chained, leaves the first "N"-device via pins 5 and 6 on the connector and is wired inside the socket to pins 1 and 2 on the next "N"-connector to the left. If the next connector is a "F"-connector it is the last element in this daisy-chain, receiving service on pins 1 and 2. That's why a dandling "N"-cable would break the chain.

With modems, there's another complication regarding this daisy-chain. As modems are commonly connected to the "N"-socket, they need to keep the chain closed in inactive state, so the voice device can receive a signal. On older, standards conforming modems, this is usually realized with a relay. You can hear this relay click any time such a modem "picks up" and goes "off hook", breaking the voice line while it's active. Newer modems, around the year 2000, often started to omit this relay for cost. A "bridged cable" or "bridged connector" was bundled instead, where the modem connects to the service lines without the return lines, in a parallel circuit with the voice device. This is against the TAE idea and creates a stub line which introduces crackling and noise into the line. In addition, you need to be aware of the requirement for a "bridged cable" in case plugging your modem in breaks the signal to your voice device.

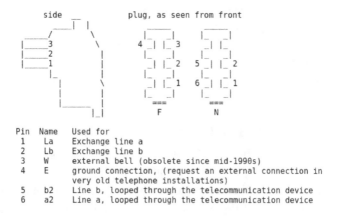

Pin	Name	Used for
1	La	Exchange line a
2	Lb	Exchange line b
3	W	external bell (obsolete since mid-1990s)
4	E	ground connection, (request an external connection in very old telephone installations)
5	b2	Line b, looped through the telecommunication device
6	a2	Line a, looped through the telecommunication device

In order to establish a connection with another modem you must know whether your modem is connected to a main line or to an extension in a private telephone system (private automatic branch exchange, PABX or PBX). Private telephone exchanges use different methods of getting a dial tone. Some require users to press the "Flash" key or you need to dial an "escape digit" (e.g. 0 or 9) to get a dial tone. You must also know if your phone company is using pulse or tone dialing. This can be determined by listening to the dialing sound. If you hear a rattling sound after each dialed number (and usually telephones using pulse dial feature a circular dial), you have pulse dialing. If you hear the touch-tone beeps when dialing, then you have tone dialing. Pulse dialing is very rare these days.

You can manually tell your modem to dial. If you're on a main line, and want to dial the example number 123456, enter ATDP123456 for pulse dialing, and ATDT123456 for tone dialing.

You probably figured out the format already. That's the opening "AT" command (mnemonic "attention!"), followed by "DT" for "dial, tone"), followed by a number. This command now is var-

ied for extension lines with a "W" for "wait for dial tone":
ATDT0 W 123456

For clarity, we here inserted spaces between "ATDT0" ("dial zero") and "W" ("wait"), followed by a number. It doesn't matter where you put spaces:

AT DT &W 123456 replaces the zero "0" with an ampersand "&" to trigger a simulated "Flash key" to get a dial tone. When dialing to an extension, or when you have issues getting a dial-tone with a line connected to a PBX system, it may be needed to tell the modem to "blind dial" without waiting for a dial-tone first. A PBX system might not provide a dial-tone although the line is already prepared to "go out". So, if you don't hear a dial tone after the Flash button or escape digit, or in any case where you have issues getting a dial-tone, you can enable "blind dialing" via the command "ATX3" (see the section on Hayes commands for the details).

ATX3DT123
Here we see multiple commands after the "AT", the "X3" for blind dialing, followed by "DT" for "dial, tone" and the number of a local branch of a PBX.

Connecting your modem to the computer

As we have learned in "What is Baud?", with a modem and using it on a computer, there are two connection lines involved in using a modem: the serial connection from your computer (and its serial port) to the modem (computer-to-modem) and the connection between the modem and some remote modem (modem-to-modem). The first connection, the local computer-to-modem connection is usually a RS232 serial connection. RS-232 is a standard for serial communication transmission of data and dates back to 1960. When people define things involved in a RS-232 serial connection, they sometimes speak of the DTE device to mean the terminal (or computer), and the DCE device, your modem. One mnemonic to tell them apart is that "DTE" contains a "T" like in "a VT100 Terminal".

That said, things moved on since the 1990s and there are USB modems, which means the common serial interface of a modem has been replaced or adapted internally with a built-in USB (Universal Serial Bus) interface on such devices, for easier connection to computers not having a COM port (anymore).

Is RS-232 the same as RS-232 C?

So you turned your modem around and on the rear DB9 or DB25 connector there's a label stating that it is a RS232C serial port (and it's usually a "female" connector with sockets, not pins). So where's the difference between RS232C and RS232? The answer is, there's no real difference, the "C" just denominates the revision of the RS232 standard that is the basis for this connector. As RS232 dates back to the 1960, the standard has seen various revisions, from RS-232-A, to RS-232-B and then RS-232-C. The most important thing that changed across these revisions is the line voltage. The original RS232 operated on 25 Volts, later revisions also accepted 12 Volts and then even 5 Volts. But devices communicating in RS-232 C still need to be tolerant to signals of 25 Volts - although they may accept lower Voltages. That means that serial adapters commonly used to connect developer boards like the Arduino or ESP8266 can't be used. These usually operate on what is commonly said to be "TTL levels" ("logic levels"), meaning they operate on Voltages below 5 Volts or 3.3 Volts, and very often aren't protected against higher Voltages and might burn on a RS232 connection. They would need what is called a "level-shifter" to communicate via RS-232. In turn, devices advertising to use RS-232-C often just use the Voltage the device as a whole operates on, like 9V, the voltage available to the line driver circuit. But some RS-232 driver chips have inbuilt circuitry to produce a different voltage just for the serial line. For the actual data transmission, voltage levels aren't really important, as long as the receiving hardware is able to discern the difference between mark and space signals above the noise floor on the wire.

On computers the RS232 [www.micropolis.com/support/kb/micropolis-robot-ics-primer#RS232] interface is usually called the COM port (for "communication") and named COM1, COM2, etc. As RS-232 specifications are formally being harmonized with the CCITT standard ITU-T/CCITT V.24, it is also often called "V.24". On old Hayes modems the RS232 connector was labeled "DTE interface".

Serial connections are usually done with cables having a DB-9 or DB-25 connector. A computer, the DTE device, normally features a "male" connector (with pins). DCE devices, like modems, usually come with "female" connectors, having sockets. Some modems, especially later and smaller models, used a circular 9-pin connector to save space. But connectors in general may vary. Even the gender on DB-9 connectors may vary. You can use a Voltmeter to confirm which side of the communication connection you are looking at: measure pin 3 and 5 of a DB-9 connector. Getting a voltage of -3V to -15V means the connector is on a DTE device. Getting such a voltage on pin 2 means you're looking at a DCE device.

A *DB-25 connector* with 25 pins is actually the "original" serial connector. It features additional connectors for additional "metadata" about the data connection, for example on pins 15, 17 and 24 a clock signal is conveyed, which is used only for synchronous communications. One important difference is that Signal Ground is on pin 7 on DB-25 connectors and on DB-9 connectors it is on pin 5.

What is a simple Straight-Through serial cable, and what a Null-Modem cable?

A *straight-through serial cable* (sometimes called a "one to one" cable) is usually used between your computer and your modem. Straight-Through is the cable type that by definition is used to connect a DTE device (PC) to a DCE device (a modem or some other communications device). The name refers to how the wires in such a cable are connected: on a straight-through cable the transmit and receive lines are *not* cross-connected, but, you already guessed it, "straight through". If you look at the schematic of such a connection, you'll notice that it is "mirror symmetrical". A straight through cable is just an extension of the connector on a device, the cable connector on the other end of the cable has the same pinout as the connector on the device.

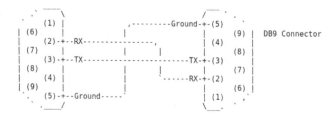

A *Null Modem cable* (sometimes called a "crossover" cable) is used to connect two DTE devices (two computers, for example)

together. As such it is commonly found in early home computer multi-player applications, where two computers, like Amigas or so, could be connected to talk to each other. A Null modem cable does what normally, in a proper serial communication situation, would happen: it connects the Transmit ("TX", or "TxD") pin of one device to the Receive ("RX", or "RxD") pin of another device, so that signals sent from one device reach the other as incoming, received signal, and vice versa. It is also the cabling needed when things like a USB serial adapter are used to talk to a development board, like an Arduino or ESP8266. It's the standard scenario when devices actually talk to each other. A straight-through cable is just an extension cord use to "relocate" a connector on a device somewhere else.

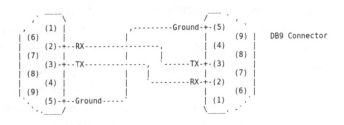

As a straight-through cable is just an "extension cord", you can attach a Null modem cable to a straight-through cable to turn the whole cable into a null modem cable with crossed lines. And in contrast to a Null Modem cable, serial cables shipped with common analog telephone modems of the 1990s were usually of the "straight-through" cable type.

A little more involved is the more complete wiring of a *Null Modem cable with handshake*. Nearly all pins of a DB-9 connector are connected through here. That's because Hardware Handshaking between devices is done via additional pins that need to be connected through. The "Request to Send" (RTS) pin of one device is then connected to the "Clear to Send" (CTS) pin of the other device, and the "Data Set Ready" (DSR) pin is connected to the "Data Terminal Ready" (DTR) pin of the other connector. But note that the below wiring is just one of many control pin wiring variations found in the wild.

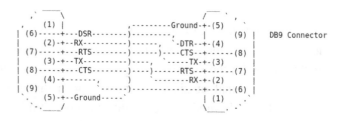

Troubleshooting a serial connection

The first thing to make sure is that your terminal application actually works. That means, confirm it can send data to your serial port. With modern systems, a serial adapter (or serial converter) is usually attached via USB. Internal serial cards are rare and motherboards with on-board UART interfaces are usually not used in an average desktop PC. So it's usually an USB dongle of sorts.

If you're on Linux, watch syslog once you connect the device (tail -f /var/log/syslog) and observe if it gets properly recognized and activated. lsusb is also a handy command to see if your serial adapter shows up. Then head over to the /dev directory and find your USB device among the TTY devices. With these small USB devices, the serial adapter is usually /dev/ttyUSB0. Note that when you do the directory listing of /dev, ls will probably displays the adapter as owned by root and as a member of the "dialout" group. Your current user usually isn't usually in group "dialout" and from that you will not have permissions to access this serial adapter. To remedy that, either add yourself to "dialout" or just change ownership of the plugged adapter:

```
$ sudo chown root: /dev/ttyUSB0
```

Once you did that and commands executed as your user have access to the adapter, you now need to confirm serial data is actually sent, with the current configuration, hardware setup and with your terminal of choice. It may happen that everything seems to be configured correctly and as if your terminal would be sending data while actually the terminal is the reason things don't get sent. So remove the terminal from the equation and set up serial in the most reduced way. For that, you can safely connect the Tx and Rx pins of the actual hardware connector, to send (or echo) data immediately back in the shortest loop possible. Check if this works by opening two command shells (terminals) side by side. In one shell fire up a simple read command, and in the other write to the socket via echo. On *nix systems everything is a file, and you can write to the serial TTY device socket just as you would to a normal file-system file.

```
$ cat /dev/ttyUSB0
```

and

```
$ /bin/echo -n -e "AT\r\n" > /dev/ttyUSB0
```

The result must be that you see the above "AT" string round-tripping and coming back as echo. Send it once, get it once. Unplug the wire-shortcut and confirm that the "AT" now does not arrive in the shell where your cat command is reading the socket. In this example we used "AT" as this is the most basic

Hayes modem command, and in case you already have a modem connected and your connection works, you should see your "AT" echoed by the modem and acknowledged with "OK". Once that works, you can continue and use a more elaborate terminal application but only when you're able to repeat this simple procedure, your terminal is actually working and able to write to the socket. This bare bones test can be a first step when everything else fails.

When connecting older modems to modern computers, you quite probably use some cheap serial adapter. If things aren't working, it might be that your adapter isn't able to discern the voltage changes which form the signals on the serial bus connection. Many serial adapters are designed for use with developer boards and expect to work with low TTL voltages of up to 5 volts. Modems usually use RS-232 connections and they may operate at higher voltages. So either your adapter will get fried by RS232 voltage levels or it may not be fit to read the serial signals on the wire. Many modems run on 9Volts and quite often the serial interface uses the same voltage. While some TTL serial adapters may tolerate 9 volts, it's better to get a proper RS-232 serial adapter.

As said above, you can measure a serial connection with a Voltmeter and see common voltages on the signaling pins - which is useful to determine the voltage level a serial communication operates on and to determine if you are looking at the DTE or DCE side of a connection. DTEs normally feature a male connector, while DCEs usually feature a female connector. As this might not always be the case, we here measure. The aim is to find out on which line the voltage is more negative, on Tx or on Rx.

On a DB-9 connector: Connect the black multi-meter lead ("minus") to pin 5, which is signal ground. Then connect the read wire ("plus"). Connect red to pin 3 and see if you get a voltage more negative than -3V. In this case, it's a DTE device. If not, measure pin 2 - if you get this lower than -3V voltage there, it's a DCE device.

For a DB-25 connector: Connect the black multi-meter lead ("minus") to pin 7, which is signal ground. Then connect the read wire ("plus"). Connect red to to pin 2 see if you get a voltage more negative than -3V. In this case, it's a DTE device. If not, measure pin 2 - if you get this lower than -3V voltage there, it's a DCE device.

Some modems may not "answer" on the local computer-to-modem serial connection without a hardware handshake first. Read more on what "hardware handshaking" is below, but for here it is only important to understand that this means additional pins on the serial wire need to be connected through on the wire and additional pins on the computer's (or adapter's) connector need to be controlled by the computer. While serial cables shipped with modems are usually fully wired, the control of all the pins on a DB-9 DTE connector may be incomplete. It depends on the driver controlling the serial port and it also depends on the serial adapter implementation if the terminal is able to properly control turning specific pins ON and OFF. The terminal must be ale to send the RTS and DTR signals. That said, in reality this should be a rare issue and your local serial connection to your modem should work without hardware handshaking.

If you connected your modem and either no "AT" commands are recognized or all you get back is garbled chars, then try setting a different Baud rate on the port talking to your modem. The DTE rate of your communications program must be set to a value within the speed range recognized by your modem. Usually modems support speed detection on the local connection. If something doesn't look right, restart the modem and your serial port and set a low bit rate first. In day to day operation though, modems usually try to match the local DTE rate to the outgoing DCE rate - but they usually support higher bit rates on the local connection and speed rates on the local and outgoing connections may be set individually.

What is the speed of the serial connection between Computer and Modem?

As described above, the serial line between the computer and your modem is a little different from the line (usually a phone line) between your modem and the outer world. Your modem is connected to your computer on an appropriate asynchronous communication interface (or "COM port") of your PC. Most modems usually harmonize the serial communication between computer and modem to match the speed on the other side, between this modem and the remote modem but the local data line may operate at higher data rates than the modem-to-modem connection and the local serial line usually doesn't use elaborate compression schemes. Speed on the local serial line depends on the capabilities of the computer's COM port. One central component of the COM port is the UART chip ("UART" is short for "Universal asynchronous receiver-transmitter". This chip manages the actual handling of getting signal-encoded bits on the wire. For modem operation during the 1990s, modem manufacturer usually recommended the COM port to use at least an UART chip of type 16550. Earlier UART chips didn't have an on-chip buffer and required the host system to pay attention to the serial communication more frequently ("IRQ interrupts").

This usually became an issue with data rates above 9600 bps on systems of the time. The popular and eponymous National Semiconductor 16550 UART chip had a 16-byte FIFO ("first in, first out") buffer and thus could handle chunks of serial data on its own, offloading work from the host system. Without a buffering UART chip, the serial connection couldn't operate error-free or without data loss at higher interface data rates. With a buffering UART, communication with modems of the era could usually be established at up to 115200 Baud.

Most modems support *autobaud* on the DTE to DCE computer-to-modem connection. That means the modem will automatically detect the speed the connected computer is trying to communicate with. Autobaud is a process where the receiving device tries to determine the employed frame length of the transmitter, deducting the used Baud rate. Autobaud is made simpler for the modem by the Hayes command set. Hayes commands all start with the "attention" string "AT" and by clever coincidence the ASCII letters "A" and "T" have a simple binary form where a binary "1" is at the beginning and the end, effectively marking the start and end of a data frame. These boundaries are easy to measure and the receiving device can adjust speed from this measurement.

Handshaking (Flow Control)

Devices communicating use some form of telling each other when they are ready and how they'd like to communicate. This is usually called "Handshaking". With serial communication, "handshaking" is also called "Flow Control". With serial communication, the main purpose of handshaking is to tell the other side when the receiving end is ready to receive data or when the sending side should stop sending and wait for the local receiver

46

to process received data. This way the interfaces prevent data from being dropped due to overloading of one end. Handshaking may happen in hardware, in software or as a combination, in both.

Software flow-control uses special codes, transmitted in-band, over the primary communications channel. These codes are generally called XOFF and XON (from "transmit off" and "transmit on", respectively). Thus, "software flow control" is sometimes called "XON/XOFF flow control". To control data flow, the receiver sends special control characters to tell the transmitter to pause sending. XON, for example, is an unprintable ASCII character ("Device Control 1", "DC1") and usually not used for text, but it is decimal 17 and hexadecimal 11 and may be used in a binary transmission and lead to data corruption when not handled properly.

Hardware handshaking or *hardware flow-control* uses dedicated out-of-band signals, means it uses actual separate hardware data lines on the RS-232 connection separate from the TX/RX lines. On pin 4, labeled as "Request to Send" ("RTS"), the transmitter sends a signal to the receiver. On pin 5, labeled "Clear to Send" ("CTS"), the receiver sends a signal to the transmitter, indicating "yes, ready". Normally, these pins are "on" throughout a communication session. "On" means this pin is set to (logic) "High". In some terminal applications, you can toggle these pin states of your COM port / serial interface manually for debugging purposes. On Linux, this is done through the ioctl() system calls. A typical handshake looks like this: the DTE (your PC, for example) likes to send data and asks for permission by setting its RTS output to high. No data will be sent until the DCE (for example, your modem) signals back that it grants permission by setting the CTS line high. This may change during a session whenever this "ready state" changes on one end, for example to process data or a buffer is full. A more general signaling mechanism is exchanged on the "DTR" ("Data Terminal Ready") and "DSR" pins ("Data Signal Ready") where connected devices signal general readiness. DSR and DTR are usually in one state, high or low, for a whole connection session. Specifically reserved for modems are pins 1 and 9. Pin 1 is "DCD" ("Data Carrier Ready") and is high whenever a modem has established a connection with remote equipment. Pin 9 is "RI" ("Ring Indicator") and the equivalent of the bell ringing on a telephone - it is set to high when a call comes in. Especially older modems have LED indicators on their front-panels indicating the status of these pins, of these "flags" of the ready-state mechanisms.

What about USB Modems?

Around the year 2000, manufacturers went from traditional RS-232 serial connected devices to modems with an in-built USB interface. This is more convenient not only due to the USB bus being easier to handle and operate but it also allowed to power modems via the bus. This way the additional cord to a wall-wart power supply became obsolete and cable wrangling got easier.

On Linux and in /var/log/syslog, USB analog modems may show up as TTY device /dev/ttyACM0 and the system will run them via the cdc_acm USB ACM device interface driver, the "USB Abstract Control Model driver for USB modems and ISDN adapters". Permission issues, group membership, etc. on the TTY device are the same as with a serial connected device, though.

Is it possible to connect two modems "back to back"?

It is possible to connect two modems locally, "back to back", meaning with a cable that directly connects the telephone line connectors on each modem, so you have a local link, without a "round trip" over your telephone company. The difference to the connection provided by your phone company is that this wire between your modems has no base voltage applied. This is called a "dry line". If this works depends on your modem. If it doesn't, you can attach a simple supply voltage to the line and simulate a proper telephone line. Another option is to use a local PBX system where you call extension numbers locally. In summary, it's a bit of a DIY project, but it is doable.

There are also commercial products to connect telephones or modems without a real telephone line, for local debugging or testing. Popular solutions are the Viking DLE-200B, product description here [vikingelectronics.com/products/dle-200b/], the Teltone TLS-4 Phone Line Simulator and the Chesilvale TSLS and TSLS2 Dual Standard Telephone Switching and Line Exchange Simulator.

Another scenario for two modems directly connected is when a "leased line" is used. A leased line, your own "copper pair", is a private telecommunications circuit between two or more locations and is either provided by a telephone company or privately operated. Such private circuits or data lines sometimes resemble a local "dry line" and vendors sell special modems to establish data link connections on such infrastructure. Some home user modems are still switchable between modes for use on a line with voltage on it and a mode for "dry lines". Modems for private circuits are still widely used and their communication standards developed far beyond the point where common analog modems for home use stagnated around the year 2000. Modern leased line modems are comparable with VDSL or ADSL modems used as broadband terminators in private homes.

Any good telephone numbers I can call? To test my modem?

You can call the US National Institute of Standards and Technology (NIST) and US Naval Observatory (USNO). They provide time services, with accurate data from their atomic clocks, which can be polled via modem at 9600bps:

```
NIST:
+1 (303) 494-4774 (Boulder, CO)
+1 (808) 335-4721 (Hawaii)

USNO:
+1 (202) 762-1594 (Washington, DC)
+1 (719) 567-6743 (Colorado Springs,
                   CO)
```

Also, the Telnet BBS Guide [www.telnetbbsguide.com/] can be filtered on BBS with dial-up nodes available.

Using an analog modem over a Voice-over-IP line

In an effort to streamline communication infrastructure in-line with advances in technology, telephone companies and telephone infrastructure operators are implementing principles of the so-called Next-Generation Network (NGN) across their installations. NGN is a body of key architectural changes in telecommunication core and access networks and aims to unify traditionally diverse infrastructure and standards into one network that is able to transport video, audio/voice and data encapsulated as IP packets over service agnostic networking infrastructure.

Many of the changes introduced as part of this effort go unnoticed by a broader audience and are implemented on the backend or backbone side of telecommunication operations. One innovation that came to end-user visibility was the introduction of all-digital phone-lines (ISDN) around the year 1990. More recently, TelCos began rolling out IP-based phone lines, known as Voice-over-IP (VoIP) that introduced an abstract way of handling calls from A to B. The "Plain old telephone system" (POTS) was built on the idea that a phone line more or less connects two parties by some physical means. This was how it was from the late 19th century and remained mostly unchanged up until 1990, despite the introduction of DTMF tone dialing (vs. pulse dialing), the introduction of ISDN or migration towards fiber-optic communication on backbones of the "public switched telephone network" (PSTN). With VoIP these direct links begin to vanish and are replaced by virtual networks, where "calls" and connections are freely routable between endpoints that are generic data routing terminals instead of service-centered analog voltage operated wall sockets.

An analog modem is a device that is deeply rooted in how analog phone lines work. It relies on the real-time nature of analog phone communication over a traditional PSTN line. It is built to compensate common analog line defects and optimized to work over a medium that was originally conceived to transport the human voice, saturating its bandwidth in a way that maxed out what is possible on such a channel. A Voice-over-IP line is a transport channel that is not optimal for an analog modem. When audio is transported via VoIP, an IP network is effectively transporting chunks of audio recordings from one end to another. That means audio is recorded and then fed through an audio codec that employs data reduction by lossy compression and bandwidth optimizations tuned for the spoken word. These packets of compressed audio are then transferred via UDP (User Datagram Protocol) that trades simplicity for reliability. The effect is that packets may get lost, are then repeated and in addition may arrive in arbitrary order. While such drawbacks are okay for simple voice communication, for modem communication, this is a show-stopper, as a modem requires exact timings.

Similar as with the introduction of energy-saving fluorescent light tubes, VoIP has a reputation of being low quality voice communication. This impression is a left-over from the early times of VoIP where network bandwidth was small and early VoIP customer lines utilized similarly small bandwidths around 16kbs. Also, speech compression codecs were less advanced. This, in combination with digital artefacts, like lacking synchronization, make VoIP problematic for analog modems. This has since changed as premium VoIP operators are increasing the allotted bandwidth for customers to over 64kbps. Also, new codecs are rolled out, some specifically tailored to analog modems signaling over VoIP, where time-stamping guarantees that chunks of recorded audio arrive timely and in order. But although things have improved, it is good to keep in mind that modem communication over VoIP has issues, may require specific VoIP settings and may not work at datarates over around 9600bps and 14.400bps.

As a note, the same is true for Fax sending. A fax is, depending on what is agreed between fax machines in a fax handshake, usually sent at data-rates between 4800bps and 33.600bps (G3 FAX). And as fax falls back on low datarates in case of trouble, the thing you would only notice is that it takes longer for a fax to go through and copies arrive in lower quality, with visible artifacts of transmission errors.

Some VoIP routers allow to configure the VoIP parameters. Units like the Cisco / Linksys PAP2 offer to edit the VoIP parameters. In case you are able to, try setting the employed VoIP codec to be either G.711/ulaw ("mu-law") or G.711/A-law and turn off all echo cancellation (silence suppression) and detection options. Also, some providers may be able to adjust "packet jitter" on a per-customer basis. If so, try asking for lower packet jitter. On the mentioned PAP2 device, there's a shorthand feature: prefix a call with "*99" and the unit toggles the line to modem settings, for fax or analog modem communication (same as doing in settings: force dtmf inband, echo cancel off, echo suppression off, silence suppression off, force g.711/ulaw, call waiting off).

Some terminology:

ATA - short for "Analog Telephone Adapter". A device to connect a traditional analog telephone or fax machine to a Voice-over-IP telephony network. The above mentioned Linksys PAP2 is such an ATA, the Cisco VG202XM or Patton SmartNode SN200/1JS are similar devices for commercial/office use. These devices simulate a traditional (POTS) line connection by providing appropriate power, a dial tone, ring generator etc. for an old-skool phone. An ATA translates the analog signaling of a telephone into a digital IP based VoIP datastream. *FXS* - short for "Foreign eXchange Station". The FXS connector on an ATA, or the FXS interface, is the connector meant to accept the cord of an analog telephone. It's where the ATA does its magic, where it provides power, signaling and analog tone to make a traditional phone work. It is the analog side of the ATA device.

FXO - short for "Foreign eXchange Office". FXO is the connector meant to be connected to a land line. In the olden days of POTS, a FXO was the interface that terminates the foreign exchange line at the central office (meaning the infrastructure of your phone company) for your phone. It's the side of the ATA where the phone number is provided and from where incoming calls are signaled inbound. The FXO terminology carried over from the days of POTS but is still used in Voice-over-IP telephony. From the point of view of a telephone exchange (your phone company), an FXO appears to be a telephone, although your "telephone" might in reality be a conglomerate of an FXO connected ATA that is translating the incoming digital VoIP calls via the FXS port for an analog telephone.

What is the Hayes Command Set?

Hayes commands are usually described in all capital letters, but modems will treat them case-insensitive.

Note that commands may be combinations of letters AND special chars, like "&" (ampersand) and "-" (minus). This can be puzzling as they might be interpreted as they usually are in language, as combinatory markers, but with Hayes commands they are part of the command! So the command "ATH0" (hang-up) is NOT the same as "AT-H0" (set modem into "dumb mode"). Some commands may omit the trailing number, for example both "ATH0" and "ATH" triggers the modem to hang-up.

For clarity, users may introduce spaces between commands. These are usually ignored by the modem. AT - issues on its own, the modem will reply with "OK" if everything's fine

```
ATH1 - pick up "the receiver" (go
       "off-hook")
ATH0 - hang-up (go "on-hook")

ATA  - answer an incoming call ("yes,
       pick up")

Command suffix "X": dialing behavior:
ATX0 - ignore dial tone / busy tone
ATX1 - ignore dial tone / busy tone
ATX2 - wait for dial tone / ignore
       busy tone
ATX3 - ignore dial tone / evaluate
       busy tone
ATX4 - wait for dial tone / evaluate
       busy tone

With ATX2 or ATX4 the modem waits for
a dial tone before dialing. With
ATX0, ATX1 or ATX3 the modem does not
wait for the dial tone, so that
"blind dialing" is possible, e.g.
while establishing a connection
between two extensions.

ATL0 - low speaker volume
ATL1 - low speaker volume
ATL2 - medium speaker volume
ATL3 - maximum speaker volume

ATM0 - speaker always off
ATM1 - speaker on when dialing and
       while waiting for answer tone
ATM2 - speaker always on
```

ATM3 - speaker on when waiting for
        answer tone

ATT - use tone dialing
ATP - use pulse dialing

Command Suffix "I": display product
information: (returned info may be
manufacturer dependent)
ATI0 - Display product code in nnn
        format
ATI1 - Display checksum
ATI2 - Display checksum result
ATI3 - Display firmware version and
        date
ATI4 - Display current configuration
        profile
ATI5 - Display serial number
ATI6 - Display product name
ATI7 - Display result of self-test
ATI9 - Display Plug and Play
        information

AT&F - Restore factory defaults

To store configuration, modems usually have internal memory
registers. Accessing and modifying these is used to modify the
configuration of the modem. The ATS command is used to toggle specific settings. For example "ATS0=3" will set the decimal number of register 0. Note that changing the value of a bit-
mapped register can affect several functions at once! That's due
to the way bit-map registers work. One register is one byte,
with decimal values from 0-255. But the modem uses the binary form of how these numbers are represented, in zeros and
ones. Most configuration options are exposed to the user
through their own dedicated AT command and you don't have

to dig around in the memory registers to toggle settings, but some need be set via registers. For example ATS0 is the register where the number is stored for after how many rings the modem should pick up. You can query a register by appending a question mark. The modem will output the current setting's decimal number then, not the bit-map.

```
ATS0    - Number of rings to auto-
          answer
ATS0?   - Read register 0 (rings to
          answer) (default usually 0)
ATS0=3 - Set register: answer incoming
          calls after 3 rings
```

What is ASCII?

ASCII, abbreviated from "American Standard Code for Information Interchange", is a character encoding standard for electronic communication designed in the 1960s for teleprinters and telegraphy, and early computing. At that time it wasn't fully fixed how many bits would be used to store information in binary electromechanical and microprocessor controlled machinery and memory storage was precious. Systems usually processed one character at a time and one bit-code had to be used to store one character. Over time 5-bit and 6-bit schemes were used and arrived at a 7-bit scheme which was able to store 128 codes, of which 33 were used for control codes (such as cursor positioning and paper feed) and 95 selected printable characters (94 glyphs and one space). These codes are usable to represent English as it covers numbers and the Latin alphabet but not much more.

This limited set of characters didn't impose a large problem for English, but for other languages, especially those using accented letters. The results was that modified ASCII variants appeared, the first local "code pages" (a term coined by IBM), that included letters or glyphs used in other languages. The original ASCII thus is usually named USASCII.

From 7-bit ASCII to 8-bit ASCII (Extended ASCII)

When computers and peripherals standardized on eight-bit bytes in the 1970s, the added bit offered the chance to store more codes into a single byte than before. It was agreed to store the original ASCII codes into the lower codes and continue to 256 codes above that. This would allow ASCII to be used unchanged, stored as 8-bit bytes with the MSB set to 0, and provide 128 more characters, a superset of ASCII, or so-called "Extended ASCII". 128 additional characters are a lot less limiting in comparison to the original 44 printable chars, but still not enough to cover all language and mathematical purposes, so, as with original ASCII, the emergence of many proprietary and national ASCII-derived 8-bit character sets was inevitable. And all of these 8-bit character sets which had more than the original 7-bit ASCII set are called extended ASCII. There is no single "extended ASCII set."

Hewlett-Packard released the "HP Roman Extensions" for use in their workstations, terminals and printers, among them "HP Roman-8" and "HP Roman-9". Atari and Commodore Business Machines added graphic symbols to their non-standard ASCII, commonly called ATASCII and PETSCII (the latter derived from the name of the Commodore PET). IBM added 8-bit extended ASCII codes on the original IBM PC. IBM called this and many other localized extensions "code pages" and in usual IBM fashion began assigning numbers to their own code pages as we as many used by other manufacturers. Accordingly, character sets are very often indicated by their IBM code page number which do share that the lower 128 codes are normal US-ASCII. DOS computers built for the North American market, for example, used code page 437 (or cp437), which adds some accented and Cyrillic characters, sprinkled with some graphical line-drawing characters for basic box graphics for good measure.

When things started to get standardized, ISO released its own extended ASCII set, ISO/IEC 8859-1, which was based on the "Multinational Character Set (MCS)" used by Digital Equipment Corporation (DEC) in their VT220 terminal. As such, it offered many accented characters but no basic graphic glyphs anymore. Microsoft then started to include the Windows-1252 charset, which was a slightly modified superset of 8859-1. Both of these are, due to their widespread use, very commonly associated with the term "extended ASCII", although still no single extended ASCII set exists.

Graphical user interfaces like Windows had rendered graphic glyphs in character sets obsolete and the effect was that dominating charsets focused on accents and mathematical symbols that were needed to represent language and science in DTP software and desktop applications. Still, around that time, the late 1980s and during the 1990s - even to this day - console applications were (and still are) heavily used. And these applications, whether it be terminal applications like popular Norton Commander or Unix/Linux terminal applications, sometimes based on curses or ncurses, still require a character set that defined pseudo-graphical glyphs that were usable for simple frame drawing and on-screen graphics. The original VT100 hardware terminal had the Special Graphics Characters [vt100.net/docs/vt100-ug/chapter3.html#T3-9] charset that defined a checkered block and elements to draw rectangles on screen. Probably stemming from there, early home computers, like the Commodores and Ataris had block drawing glpyhs in their PETSCII and ATASCII charsets. The equivalent of these character sets in the DOS console world was IBM's "OEM font" CP437 mentioned above. It was used to draw many text-mode GUIs, and probably most important, the DOS-based demo, crack and ANSIart "scene" embraced this charset. "ANSI"-BBS Boards used the frames and blocks extensively. One example is the "hatched" or "checkered" block character. As said, the VT100 had one and its intentional use was to indicate an error. Commodore PETSCII charsets also had one, but IBM's CP437 had three of such blocks, and in stepped opacity, allowing artists to draw simple gradient shadings with them. In combination with color, CP437 fostered remarkable creativity. Modern BBSs of today still use CP437 but the original CP437 charset may be UTF-8 encoded. As UTF-8 is perfectly capable to represent all common char code points, layouts and artworks look just the same.

All of these codepages and custom character sets were largely replaced and/or subsumed by UTF-8 multi-byte character encoding. UTF-8 is different from ASCII but also a superset and backwards compatible. UTF-8 isn't Unicode either. UTF-8 is a variable-length character encoding where one to four one-byte (8-bit) code units represent a character by encoding its "code point", the numeric value mapped to a char. UTF-8 is backwards compatible with ASCII because UTF-8 tries to be as terse as possible and the first 128 characters of Unicode, which correspond one-to-one with ASCII, are encoded using a single byte with the same binary value as ASCII, so that valid ASCII

60

text is valid UTF-8-encoded Unicode as well. Note: Although the official spelling of "UTF-8" includes a hyphen, it is sometimes written without it or with space instead of the hyphen, "utf8" or "UTF 8".

Modern terminal emulations usually are capable of receiving and "understanding" UTF-8 and will display even esoteric characters with a high code point correctly. Specials chars used for semigraphic drawing in CP437 are then encoded as their UTF-8 equivalent. That said, it doesn't matter so much as most Western "character mode" systems, including BBS, use predominantly characters from the traditional ASCII character set and the fact that a received data stream is actually UTF-8 encoded will only show occasionally when a wide char is encountered and an utf-8 encoded multi byte sequence reaches the terminal. In a non-utf8-capable terminal such a byte sequence would just show as garbled or unprintable chars but won't do more harm than that - a slight glitch in display.

What is ANSI

"ANSI encoding" is a generic term and has been used to refer to many different things. ANSI normally is just the abbreviation for "American National Standards Institute", but there is no "ANSI encoding" or "code page" and the term doesn't correspond to any actual ANSI standard - only the name has stuck.

The term "ANSI" may refer to "ANSI escape code sequences", an in-band signaling mechanism for terminals and terminal emulators, or "ANSI BASIC programming language standards" used to denominate different evolutions of the BASIC programming language, but most prominently "ANSI" refers to an "ANSI character set" - either "Windows-1252" or "Code page

437". In Microsoft Windows world the Windows-1252 character set is often nicked "ANSI" due to a historically grounded misnomer. On the other hand, "CP437" is probably the most prominent character set being named the "ANSI character set", at least in the context of Bulletin Board Systems (BBS) and "ANSI art". In these contexts either the "extended ASCII" charset or much more often CP437 with its block drawing glyphs is used, oftentimes mixed wth "ANSI escape sequences" that color character glyphs with the 16 foreground and 8 background colors offered by ANSI.SYS, an MS-DOS device driver loosely based upon the ANSI X3.64 standard for text terminals. For an in-depth description on ANSI escape codes read on further down.

What are ANSI escape codes? And how do these code sequences work?

An escape sequence is a defined sequence of printable and/or unprintable characters (control characters). An escape character is a character that invokes an alternative interpretation on the following characters in a character sequence. Generally, the judgment of whether something is an escape character or not depends on context, which is usually a "standard" or "norm" defined for some application - here it is the context of terminals and emulation thereof. Escape sequences allow moving the cursor to an arbitrary position on screen (or historically paper output), clearing portions of the screen, changing colors and displaying special characters, and also, in turn, signal the pressing of function keys, cursor or other special keys or combinations of keys, like the CTRL-C break signal.

"ANSI escape codes" are a different thing from "Telnet commands" and "Telnet's IAC" (interpret as command) code sequences. Both, in a way, interact with the terminal or its display but ANSI escape codes mainly refer to the presentation of content in a terminal, while Telnet commands are used to communicate with the terminal *itself*. Refer to the section on Telnet for an explanation of Telnet commands.

Note that while discussing ASCII control characters and ANSI escape codes, a notation known as "caret notation" is used often. The notation assigns ^A ("caret" + "A") to "control-code 1", sequentially through the alphabet to ^Z assigned to "control-code 26" (0x1A). For control-codes outside of the range 1–26, the notation extends to the adjacent, non-alphabetic ASCII characters, like the "at sign" ("@") for code "0" (NUL), expressed as "^@" or code 27 (ESC) written as "^[". Often a control character can be typed on a keyboard by holding down the CTRL-key and typing the character shown after the caret. Try it in your terminal of choice: type a few letters, then hold down CTRL and press "H". The preceding chars will get deleted, as ^H is the control code for "BACKSPACE".

There are a number of "classes" of control codes, ordered by their complexity/length, these are:

C0

C0 control codes are the most rudimentary ANSI escape codes and are all just a single byte long. Initially these were defined as part of ASCII and they provide the basic actions of a printer or display. To emit a carriage return command (CR), the code "^M" is used, hexadecimally this is equivalent to "0x0D". A line feed (LF) is triggered with "^J" (hex "0x0A"), the escape key is triggered by "^[". This means (caret notation): "press CTRL and square left bracket" to emit the special char for ES-

CAPE (which is the char "0x1B" in hexadecimal notation). This char is especially interesting, as it starts all the ANSI escape sequences and is the reason these sequences are named accordingly. Note that there are other notations for expressing the unprintable char "ESC". But these expressions do not describe a key combination you can press on the keyboard but are a presentational shorthand or a special string that some programming languages interpret as a description of a hexadecimal value. For example "backslash and e" instead of a caret, so you'd write "\e[". Other languages allow an even more condensed notations where you can write "backslash plus "x", like this "\x1B", for a hex value or the octal number equivalent of a binary value with a backslash, like so "\033[".

Fe

Fe Escape sequences are the first "real" control codes in our context here as they are formed by a two-byte sequence. The first byte, representing the ESC key, which we've learned to emit above, if this ESC byte is immediately followed (in the data stream) by a byte in the hex range 0x40 to 0x5F, then this escape sequence is of type "Fe". What it means depends on the applicable C1 control code standard, which is defined in ANSI standard X3.64 (ECMA-48) and we here can just ignore Fe sequences for now.

CSI

Much more interesting in our context, as they are used in BBS, are CSI (Control Sequence Introducer) sequences. For "Control Sequence Introducer", or "CSI", commands, the ESC is followed by any number (including none) of "parameter bytes" in the range 0x30–0x3F (ASCII 0–9:;<=>?), then by any number of "intermediate bytes" in the range 0x20–0x2F (ASCII space and !"#$%&'()*+,-./), then finally by a single "final byte" in the range 0x40–0x7E (ASCII @A–Z[\]^_`a–z{|}~). These sequences are used to encode (or emit) cursor keys, erasing the display, positioning the cursor on the screen or requesting a "device status report" with "CSI 6n", in escaped hex string notation this would be "\x1b[6n", in caret notation "^[6n". Sending the "device status report" CSI code "DSR" triggers that the remote terminal sends a CPR back (cursor position report) by transmitting "^[n;mR", where "n" is the numeric row, "m" is the column, the semicolon a separator and "R" the report "final byte" or terminator. Once again, in simpler words: CSI sequences are always composed of the ESC-byte followed by the "left square bracket"-byte and end with some letter. In-between may be a single number or multiple numbers separated by semicolon. Missing numbers are (usually) treated as 0, and no parameters at all in "ESC[m" acts like a 0 reset code. This is useful when it comes to color, as we see next.

SGR (Select Graphic Rendition) parameters and Colors

Probably the most well-known subset of CSI sequences is the CSI code "ESC[nm", where "ESC" stands for "\x1b" and is followed by a square bracket, and where "n" is the content (attributes) of the control sequence and "m" the "final byte" end marker of the sequence which identifies this CSI as the "Select Graphic Rendition" (SGR) sequence or "SGR control sequence". Several attributes can be set in the same sequence, separated by semicolons. Each display attribute remains in effect until a following occurrence of SGR resets it. If no codes are given, "CSI m" is treated as "CSI 0 m" (reset/ normal), as explained above for missing numbers.

There is a fixed "vocabulary" of codes to control various aspects of text display. "ESC[1m", where the "code"-number is "1", is defined as "switch text to bold or increased intensity". Code 2 sets "Faint, decreased intensity, or dim", code 3 switches font into italic, 4 underlines and 5 makes text blink. Code "ESC[30m" (code "30") sets the foreground text color to black, 31 to red, 32 to green, up until 37 for white. These 8 colors form the 8 core color commands. Which color exactly "red", for example, is, depends on terminal implementation. Codes 40-47 work analogous to foreground colors and define the coloring of the text background. This way one can achieve a black on white, or inversed, text look. To reset colors, one can use the general reset sequence "ESC[m" or use the special control sequence "ESC[39m" to reset foreground text color to its default or code "49" for the same effect on text background color.

Note again that one sequence may set multiple attributes at once, for example "ESC[1;31m" (codes 1 and 31) would set "bold/bright red". Also note that many terminals began to interpret the mode "bold" in combination with one of these colors as "a brighter shade" of the base color instead of switching actual font to bold. That's why common ANSI color semigraphics exhibit 16 colors, despite the actual standard only defining eight. Later terminals like aixterm added the ability to directly specify the "bright" colors with codes 90–97 for fore- and 100–107 for background.

Computers advanced and when 256-color lookup tables became common on graphic cards, escape sequences were added to select from a pre-defined set of 256 colors. The previously unused CSI codes 38 and 48 were selected for this. The specification defined the format to be "ESC[38;5;nm" to select foreground color, where "38" is the actual CSI code, the "5" after the semicolon identifies the format following and "n" can be a number 0-255 which maps to a color table of colors derived from a 4×4×4 color cube. This improved reliability of actual presented color, but colors still differed between implementations.

For modern computers there's even a 24-bit "true color" CSI color format. If a control sequence similar to the 256 color form is used, but with a "2" instead of a "5" - then the sequence is interpreted as 24-bit color. The sequence "ESC[38;2;128;64;32m" request coloring of foreground text with RGB values of "128" for red, "64" for green and "32" for blue.

What is phreaking or blue boxing?

In broad strokes, phreaking is a slang term that describes the activity of studying and experimenting with telecommunication systems, namely the telephone. This hobby emerged due to the fact that using a phone line for data transmission meant that the line subscriber is taxed a fee for each minute the computer is on-line. People tried to avoid that and a method called "blue boxing" was at one point possible, where a person could send certain tones into the phone line to establish a connection that the phone company wouldn't include in an invoice. These sounds are similar to the tones you know from your phone if it uses "tone dialing" with DTMF tones. Legend has it that a perfect 2600 Hertz tone, whistled with a plastic toy from a cereal box, could trigger a phone to enter "operator mode". In the movie "WarGames" teenage hacker David Lightman (Matthew Broderick) uses a pull-tab from a soda-can to make a free long distance call to his girlfriend. Naturally, all of this was not legal. Neither free calls nor tinkering with the public phone system in any way. And it was only possible in a short period and largely in the US. Despite these facts, or just because of these facts, the "dream" of getting a zero-cost always-on data link continued to circulate in BBS circles and was topic of countless text magazines distributed through BBS.

What are DTMF tones?

DTMF is short for "Dual-tone multi-frequency signaling" is a telecommunication signaling system that uses the voice-frequency band to transmit simple commands to telephony equipment. DTMF tones are the tones used in telephones for tone dialling, first used in the U.S. by the Bell System. The DTMF tones are sums of two sine wave tones at following frequencies:

	1209Hz	1336Hz	1477Hz	1633Hz
		ABC	DEF	
697Hz	1	2	3	A
	GHI	JKL	MNO	
770Hz	4	5	6	B
	PRS	TUV	WXY	
852Hz	7	8	9	C
		oper		
941 Hz	*	0	#	D

What or who is the "SysOp"?

The term "SysOp" is short for "system operator" and is the person who oversees the operation of a computer system. Historically it was the person who was responsible for the operation of a mainframe computer system or other larger computer systems. Especially in the context of bulletin board systems (BBS) the term Sysop somehow stuck, probably as the heyday of BBS during the late 1970s and 1980s was a epochal nexus era between classic computing and modern days and running and administering a BBS as a relatively complex multi-user computer system was a task similar to administering a mainframe computer. A person with equivalent functions on a network host or server is typically called a sysadmin, short for system administrator. A person with responsibilities reaching into the content area of a service is usually the "webmaster".

What is a WarDialer?

Matthew Broderick's character David Lightman in John Badham's 1983 feature film "WarGames" is a computer enthusiast. He uses a modem to connect to remote computer systems. One technique he uses to find such systems is to dial every telephone number in Sunnyvale, California in order to find a line where a computers answers. In remembrance of this film, this technique is called "War Dialing" and a program used to do so is a "War Dialer". Of course, trying thousands of telephone numbers would produce a very hefty phone bill - as such, using a war dialer is often related to "phone phreaking" where people find ways to make calls for free.

War dialing is a form of brute force attack. It exchanges an educated guess of a certain outcome for a simple exploration of every possible option. In dialing, this means consecutively calling every number from a certain block, area or prefix. A similar approach can be found in port scanning to find weak systems, or in "war driving" where people drive around in cars to find Wi-Fi networks. War dialing techniques in altered form are used to this day and there are program to perform automated dialing of VoIP virtualized phone lines.

Note: Usually, a dialer is activated by the program owner, but during the era of dial-up computer networking, a common malware was a "dialer". Unsuspecting users would somehow be tricked into installing a software with embedded secret code, or a separate program would find its way on an unsuspecting user's system. Such "dialers" would then, at arbitrary times when the phone-line wasn't used, pick up the hook and dial specific numbers. It was common that people noted this from the modem suddenly becoming active and a quick reach to the manual off-switch on the backside of the modem would end the uninitiated call of the compromised system.

What is a lightbar?

Some BBSs accept user input via cursor keys. On screens with options, a preselected option is highlighted by inverting the common white on black characters to black characters on a white background. This white background is then extended beyond the actual tracking width of the characters used to describe the option, forming a whole line across a menu dialog or the whole screen width. This resembles a white bar or "lightbar". SysOps came to call this type of highlighting and a BBS's capability to offer users this kind of interactive menu a "lightbar".

Usually, it has nothing to do with the "Lightcycles" from the popular 1982 Disney movie TRON.

What are "terminal modes"?

Some Background: A lightbar menu requires that the client is in a mode that sends each character immediately after a user has pressed the respective key. Usually, with Terminals, this is not the default. Terminals commonly operate in "Line by line mode", which means everything you type as a client/user of a remote system/server on your local terminal is only sent over the wire *after* you pressed ENTER (or after you triggered an "end-of-transmission", EOT, signal, usually via ^D, CTRL-D). In "Line by line mode" the same is true for "special keys" like the cursor arrow. If you press the cursor arrows in this "line at a time"-mode, your terminal (given it is in "local echo mode", which is the default) will just display the escape sequence for arrow keys, for example "^[[C" for "arrow right".

Actually, it is not the terminal that is buffering input until encountering an ENTER, it is the tty layer of the operating system that's buffering input. More exactly a component called "line discipline [en.wikipedia.org/wiki/Line_discipline]" (LDISC). On Linux, the command stty can be used to alter the "line discipline" of the tty layer. The two modes [en.wikipedia.org/wiki/Terminal_mode] that can be toggled are called "cooked" mode, where line discipline is enabled, and "raw" mode, where it is not. "Line discipline" is a buffer that buffers all entered chars (text, commands, escape sequences) until the user hits ENTER. And only then, in "cooked" mode, line discipline would submit the buffer contents over the line to the remote terminal/system.

Historically, this was to ease load for a system processing all these user inputs. Imagine an old mainframe computer, with limited processing power, that had many terminals attached and each time someone on each terminal would press a key, the processing system would have to switch to the task of this user and process this one entry. That was inefficient and thus "line discipline" was invented. With line discipline, the system only had to switch when one complete command (or whatever was sent) came in, and not on every keystroke.

Modern computers can easily handle this load. And When "line discipline" is turned off, which means the tty layer is switched to "raw" mode, then every character and also any BACK-SPACE or navigational cursor-key keystroke, everything the user enters, is immediately sent over the wire and processed on the remote and. This is where another mode, "local echo"-mode comes in. For local editing prior to submit, the terminal obviously displays each typed char. With raw mode, where each char is immediately sent, this is usually switched off. The reason is that when the remote end is expected to immediately process each char, it may also modify each char and thus, for the user to know what happened after each char, the remote system sends each character (or whatever modified result) back. With chars, this usually looks like a "local echo" of a key press, but it may also be "just nothing" in response or, as with light-bars, something more complex. If you're interested here [www.-sobyte.net/post/2022-05/tty/]'s a more in-depth discussion of how and why all this works.

So, as we now might already understand, for lightbars to work, we need to have a terminal that's switched to "raw" mode, "no line discipline" and "local echo off". Imagine some multiple choice menu on a BBS. By means of some ASCII art or graphical chars, three options are drawn on screen. A note says you

72

may select via arrow keys. The uppermost option is selected with a "lightbar", where the text is inversed to black on white, as if this line was highlighted by some light. You now want to navigate down, to option two, and press the "arrow down"-key. By that, you trigger the ANSI escape code for "arrow down" ("^[[B"), but it isn't displayed, instead it is immediately sent to the remote system. The remote end then calculates how the menu looked before your input and alters this rendition to how it should look after your input, and then sends cursor and edit commands to your terminal, to erase portions of the menu and redraw other portions of the menu. This happens very fast and to you it appears as if the "lightbar" just moved from option one to option two. In fact, this more elaborate response was just the "echo" of your entered "arrow down"-key.

With BBS connections you probably don't think much about your TTY's mode. And that's probably because you're using Telnet to connect to BBS. BBS through Telnet isn't the same as a directly attached ANSI Terminal. And Telnet can be configured, either to behaves like a direct TTY terminal connection and use something like "line discipline" or not. Bulletin Boards in turn may operate in line-disciplined/buffered or unbuffered/raw modes, depends on how their interfaces work. Buffered is usually more compatible, as it needs to know less about the remote end. Buffered is also the "original" way terminals worked, as they tried to save resources on the remote mainframe's end - thus buffered is usually the default on *nix systems. And buffered is also the mode Telnet falls back to when the remote end doesn't respond to it's initial negotiation requests. We've already learned about Telnet IAC commands in "What is Telnet?" above. Upon connect, Telnet needs to decide what to do, thus it tries to get into a "raw"mode that sends characters at a time but will fall back to the oldest and most compatible line-wise mode if it fails.

For a "cooked" "line by line"-mode in Telnet, the old way was a "pseudo line by line"-mode called "kludge line mode" or "old line by line"-mode as it is called in telnet's man pages. It is the default and fall-back state of Telnet, and is enabled via two options in their default state: SGA (Suppress Go Ahead) is disabled, which means "Go Ahead" markers are sent/expected and ECHO is off (this is not "local echo" but "remote echo", meaning that every data character received is echoed back to remote). The RFCs which define these features, RFC 858 and 857, date back to 1983. If a client answers to the Telnet server that it agrees to (WILL) start SGA, it effectively means that from then on character at a time is in effect. Other implementations only require agreement on ECHO to leave "line at a time"-mode, while it is also common to require SGA and ECHO to be enabled for a "raw" character-at-a-time connection. If a remote server wouldn't answer the SGA and ECHO negotiation requests, telnet falls back to (or better, remains in) its default "kludge line by line"-mode.

Developers tried to overcome this kludge by a new Telnet option introduced in 1990 (RFC 11169 which defined a process to specifically configure a Telnet LINEMODE, but while it allowed more fine grained control of behavior, it's also more complicated and not as widely supported as "kludge line mode". That's why most BBS use the SGA+ECHO option, answer it correctly and switch Telnet into "raw"-mode this way.

One last note: old style communication software, the type you may encounter in retro computing, the type that has built in modem support, FOSSIL driver, phonebook and terminal emulation, etc. - these older terminals are usually set to "raw" mode by default and send everything immediately. They don't follow the Telnet specs and/or do not answer IAC markers. Unix-style terminals in contrary, or more up-to-date communication suites, where proper Telnet emulation is built-in, will act properly but also according to specs, they will revert to "line by line" when the remote end doesn't answer more specific Telnet negotiations.

Can I Telnet over the Internet, in-browser?

The first thing to understand is that one probably means by "the Internet" is what most people associate with the word "Internet": the "Word Wide Web" or "WWW". The thing you access and scour around with a "Browser". But the WWW is only one of many "Internet services" and is brought to you via a network protocol called TCP/IP and another protocol called HTTP on top of that. The mode of operation of WWW via HTTP is that a client, your browser, asks for a resource and a server, on the remote end, sends something over the network for your browser to process. This semantic is not directly compatible with how Telnet works.

While Telnet over the Internet, meaning Telnet through the networking infrastructure that is "the Internet", is perfectly possible and exactly how it works, establishing a Telnet connection via Internet-Browser is a different thing. Telnet is a relatively simple form of communication. Basically, for Telnet, a network socket is opened and both ends of the socket may send data at any given time, assuming the connection remains "open". A connection where both ends may send and/or receive at the same time is called "full duplex". HTTP communication for the WWW is usually "half duplex", where requests and responses are mutually exclusive. While communication with a Terminal may be "half duplex" to simplify things on both ends, Telnet per se is "full duplex". And facilitating proper Telnet communication over the Internet requires a protocol which overcomes the half duplex nature of common HTTP. That said, the relation to HTTP here is only stemming from the fact that the idea is to enable Telnet coming from WWW technologies, asking for Telnet-like "full duplex" communication in the Browser.

To remedy the situation of Browsers only "speaking" half-duplex protocols, a new protocol called WebSocket was invented. The WebSocket protocol was standardized by the IETF as RFC 6455 in 2011 and can be describes as an extension of HTTP, where a WebSocket handshake uses the HTTP "Upgrade" header to change from the HTTP protocol to the WebSocket protocol. A WebSocket is a connection between your browser and the remote end that remains open for extended periods of time. It is a standardized way for the server to send content to the client without being first requested by the client, and allowing messages to be passed back and forth while the WebSocket is established. This significantly reduces protocol overhead, as HTTP normally sends verbose headers with each request, and it tells connected parties that a connection is meant to remain open for a longer session, while HTTP, in its most basic form, usually closes connection after each request. As such, a WebSocket can be thought of as way to tell browsers to open a networking socket that works less like WWW and more like an old-skool plain network connection. The WebSocket protocol defines two prefixes, "ws://" and "wss://", to indicate a insecure WebSocket (means unencrypted) and its secured (encrypted) variant.

Once we have the means to establish a simple network connection that's being "kept-alive" for the whole session, we can attach some Terminal speaking Telnet to this network connection. In-Browser Telnet clients usually emulate common Terminal semantics, but instead of connecting to the network via IP socket, these Web-based HTML5 Telnet clients connect to a WebSocket to send and receive data. So in order to enable Telnet via the WWW, we need two components already: Web-Sockets and a HTML5 Telnet client, probably implemented in JavaScript. But what about the remote end? What is connected there and what is sending data through the WebSocket?

In-Browser Telnet, to connect to a BBS

While a traditional BBS is probably directly reachable with a traditional Telnet client over the Internet, we are here discussing how we can connect to a BBS without a traditional Telnet client, only with a Browser, running some emulation of Telnet. This can be desirable in situations where users can't use real Telnet clients, or in order to lower the entry barrier for novice users. It's always easier when users can use a technology they already know well, like their browser, to experience things a little more complicated, like visiting a BBS.

The Micropolis BBS [www.micropolis.com/support/kb/micropolis-bbs] is an example of a BBS that is directly reachable via the Internet, via "real" Telnet, and at the same time offers users to connect via *in-browser Telnet client* to the same BBS from the convenience of their Browsers. Once you do that, there are already three elements in action, of which we already know two: (1) a browser front-end emulation of a Telnet client, visible as a rather old-fashioned looking rectangle embedded into a website. Underlying this interface then is (2) the WebSocket technology, which allows the client to pass data in a full-duplex way to a remote service. And then there's a third element, a WebSocket adapter, or "proxy", that connects this data stream with the traditional

77

BBS Telnet service, as if a client had connected to the BBS directly. For this enumeration here, we don't regard the BBS as a fourth element, as we assume that this service is a natural prerequisite. Try a connect to the Micropolis BBS [www.micropolis.com/support/kb/micropolis-bbs] via your browser and you can experience all these elements working in unison.

How to setup in-browser Telnet for your own BBS

Setting up a Web-Frontend for a traditional BBS is not that difficult. Now that we have a good grasp of how all this works, we can setup a WebSocket based Telnet emulation on our own. Let's assume we have some BBS software package up and running on a local Linux development machine. The service is reachable via standard Telnet port 23. (That said, note that on a *nix system port 23 is regarded as a "privileged port", like all ports 0-1023, and requires the service to be either run as root (bad idea in production) or some local "port forwarding" to port 23 going on.) The next thing we then need is the adapter to translate a direct Telnet socket into a WebSocket. There are a number of so called "WebSocket servers" out there designed for generic real-time applications. The node based ws [github.com/web-sockets/ws], Socket.IO [socket.io/] and even Apache web server has a module to extend the popular server package with WebSocket capabilities. For our setup we'd like a websocket server that's designed to permit Telnet to WebSocket easily. There's fTelnet Proxy [github.com/rickparrish/fTelnetProxy] from the popular-in-BBS-circles fTelnet package or the very popular Python tool websockify [pypi.org/project/websockify/] (on github), which we'll use here.

You can install websockify via Python's pip ("pip install websockify") but it's also available as Linux package and can be installed via apt ("sudo apt install python3-websockify"). Once that is done, websockify will require an SSL certificate. It won't run without one so its easiest to just issue a self-signed certificate for our test setup here. Use openssl to do that with "openssl req -x509 -newkey rsa:4096 -keyout key.pem -out cert.pem -sha256 -days 365" and answer all questions with something generic. For "Common Name (e.g. server FQDN or YOUR name)" you can enter "127.0.0.1", your local host. This command will produce two files, cert.pem and key.pem, and we'll now use both to start our WebSocket adapter locally: "websockify 127.0.0.1:23 127.0.0.1:2323 --cert cert.pem --key key.pem". Note that the websockify docs speak of "source" and "target" in a slightly ambiguous way, as from the perspective of the adapter websockify the "source" is our local BBS port, so you might have to reverse your idea of which end is which.

Once websockify is running, it will expose a local WebSocket on port 2323, which we may express as "ws://127.0.0.1:2323". This endpoint is where we now need to connect our web frontend to. The idea of websockify, of translating WebSockets traffic to normal socket traffic, for example to feed into a BBS, has been implemented in various languages, one is pure JavaScript. The websockify-js [github.com/novnc/websockify-js] project has an example file demonstrating a web front-end setup. Another popular project is the fTelnet Browser-based web Telnet client [www.ftelnet.ca/], which we'll use here.

Build a simple HTML page and embed the fTelnet JavaScript code in it. Save the HTML page and serve it locally from a local directory, for example with "python -m SimpleHTTPServer 8080". Make sure that you update the JavaScript options of the embedded fTelnet client in HTML source according to our setup: "Options.Hostname" is '127.0.0.1' with "Options.Port" set to "2323". "Options.ProxyHostname" is also '127.0.0.1' but with "Options.ProxyPort" set to port '23', where our local BBS is listening. Open a browser and navigate to this locally served page. The fTelnet client will load and you can then connect to your local BBS via the WebSocket proxy we run via the websockify command above.

So in summary, to once again explain what's going on here, to enable Telnet via in-browser: we have a front-end web Telnet client, which connects to a WebSocket, a websocket provided by websockify, which adapts WebSocket traffic to a BBS TCP socket by translating WebSocket traffic to normal network traffic. The web front-end client then only needs to render the BBS-served content according to common BBS encodings and you get the BBS experience, only on the WWW, or in a Browser more precisely.

Further reading and material elsewhere

A phonebook with a curated list of popular or favorite BBS to call was the first thing every BBS user would have. That could be pen on paper or a small database built into your terminal communication suite of choice. As an archival endeavor, textfiles.org keeps a snapshot of all those numbers that once were reachable online at bbs.textfiles.org [bbslist.textfiles.com/]. Most of them long gone. If you want to connect to a BBS today, you can visit one of the few BBS directories on the WWW. Some offer filters to list BBS by access type, Telnet or dial-up, others curate BBS tailored for a specific retro computer system.

Online Resources

- TelnetBBSGuide [www.telnetbbsguide.com/]
- Synchronet BBS List [synchro.net/sbbslist.html]
- BBS.Guide [bbs.guide/]
- IPTIA Consulting BBS Resources [www.ipingthereforeiam.com/bbs/]
- telnet.org [www.telnet.org/htm/places.htm] has a few curated BBS services listed
- BBSLink BBS Index [bbslink.net/list.php]
- Commodore BBS [cbbsoutpost.servebbs.com/]
- BBSIndex.de [bbsindex.de/bbsstats/index.php?system=blackicebbs]

- and, of course, our Micropolis BBS [www.micropolis.com/support/kb/micropolis-bbs] at bbs.micropolis.com port 23.

Discussion

- r/bbs [www.reddit.com/r/bbs/] on reddit.com

Videos

There's a very in-depth documentary [www.bbsdocumentary.com/] about the many aspects and cultural impact of the 1980s BBS scene. Learn about the beginnings of BBS, about users and SysOps, trace the story to its commercialization, the early networks it sparked, like FidoNet or RelayNet, the artscene and underground movements - and its final replacement by a thing called the Internet.

This German video [www.youtube.com/watch?v=uKk3XZn7ZG4] demonstrates old hardware and presents a workbench setup to operate two analog modems "back to back" over a local line without dial tone and without a source of voltage (over a "dry line" or "unconditioned"). Notes on how that is done are also available in a section of the Modem How-To [tldp.org/HOWTO/Modem-HOWTO-26.html] and DIY build instructions are here and here.

Modem Links

Probably one of the most exhaustive guides on modems, their use and technical details, was written by David S. Lawyer and can be found, for example, here [tldp.org/HOWTO/Modem-HOWTO.html].

Our Handbooks Series

If you enjoyed this book, then we would like to recommend these other publications that have already appeared in the series:

- **Micropolis Data Storage Primer**
  A quick-start guide on basic concepts and advanced topics of computer data storage.
- **Micropolis Robotics Primer**
  A quick-start guide on basic concepts, mechanics and forms of (industrial) robotics.

Follow Micropolis online

You can reach Micropolis on our official website and via various social media platforms:

> https://www.micropolis.com/

On YouTube

> https://www.youtube.com/@MicropolisOfficial
> https://www.youtube.com/@MicropolisUsersGroup

On Instagram

> https://www.instagram.com/micropolis.official/

Join the Discussion on Reddit

> https://www.reddit.com/r/Micropolis/

More links and ways to connect on our website.

About Micropolis

Micropolis is a new venture, determined to breathe life into a legendary brand, a computer brand well-known for pioneering electronic and mechanical data storage systems. Under new management, Micropolis strives to live up to the high level of reliability and technical excellence past customers have come to expect, and providing new users with products they can trust on for years.

Brand Legacy

Micropolis was established as a brand in the 1970s. In a time when home-computers began to become a reality for private users. Micropolis Corporation entered the business as a manufacturer of floppy drive controller cards and, building on this early expertise, started to manufacture its own line of 5.25-inch floppy disk drives soon after.

Just as today, storage demands back then grew and customers asked for ever higher data density and reliability for their storage subsystems. Micropolis Corporation answered these demands with the introduction of "rigid disk" systems. Stemming from its experience with controller electronics and mechanical drive systems grew a line of early 8-inch hard-disk drives. In the following years, this product lineup saw miniaturization and higher capacities, with drives offered in the 5.25-inch full-height and later 3.5-inch form factor.

Twenty years after its inception, during the 1990s, the company wasn't only offering hard-disk-drives but had branched out into storage enclosures. A line of deskside "data silo"-type enclosures offered plug-in data storage, packaged in a smart and modular subsystem. But this visionary technology, which anticipated today's storage virtualization, didn't help when many competitors had entered the storage market during the decade. Despite a loyal customer base, Micropolis Corporation experienced cost pressure, was sold, restructured and ultimately, in a market shakeout, ceased operation in 1997.

Micropolis' Future

Today, over 40 years later, the computing landscape has changed dramatically. Data storage density has grown exponentially and systems have seen vast improvements in terms of capabilities and miniaturization. Time has come for a reboot. With a brand like Micropolis, which has such a deep heritage in storage, our contemporary operations will offer customers a line of products that bridge old paradigms with today's demands. Similarly as in Micropolis' first incarnation, new Micropolis will again cater to storage related use-cases and our operations will aim to live up to proven expectations of Legendary Reliability. Legendary Excellence.[SM]